other books by
Francis A. Schaeffer

Escape from Reason
The God Who Is There
Death in the City
Pollution and the Death of Man
The Church at the End of the 20th Century
The Mark of the Christian
He Is There and He Is Not Silent
True Spirituality
Genesis in Space and Time
Back to Freedom and Dignity
Basic Bible Studies
Art and the Bible
No Little People
Everybody Can Know (Francis & Edith Schaeffer)
How Should We Then Live?
Whatever Happened to the Human Race?

Joshua
and
the Flow of
Biblical
History

Francis A. Schaeffer

InterVarsity Press
Downers Grove
Illinois 60515

© 1975 by L'Abri Fellowship.

All rights reserved. No part of this book may be reproduced in any form without written permission from InterVarsity Press, Downers Grove, Illinois.

InterVarsity Press is the book-publishing division of Inter-Varsity Christian Fellowship, a student movement active on campus at hundreds of universities, colleges and schools of nursing. For information about local and regional activities, write IVCF, 233 Langdon St., Madison, WI 53703.

Distributed in Canada through InterVarsity Press, 1875 Leslie St., Unit 10, Don Mills, Ontario M3B 2M5, Canada.

ISBN 0-87784-773-8 (paper)
Library of Congress Catalog Card Number: 74-31847

Printed in the United States of America

| 20 | 19 | 18 | 17 | 16 | 15 | 14 | 13 | 12 | 11 | 10 | 9 | 8 |
| 94 | 93 | 92 | 91 | 90 | 89 | 88 | 87 | 86 | 85 | | | |

To all those younger men and women
of the next generation who
are faithful to
the first changeless factor, the written book–
especially as they take seriously
that it is what it claims to be,
the written Word of God without error,
including in all that it teaches
concerning history and the cosmos.

one
Joshua's Preparation

Joshua is an important book for many reasons—for the history it records and for its internal teaching. But what makes the book of Joshua overwhelmingly important is that it stands as a bridge, a link between the Pentateuch (the writings of Moses) and the rest of Scripture. It is crucial for understanding the unity the Pentateuch has with all that follows it, including the New Testament.

The story of the man Joshua begins not in the book of Joshua but in the book of Exodus. After the Israelites had crossed the Red Sea in their flight from Egypt, they came just a few days later to Rephidim (Ex. 17). There they began to murmur against God; Moses, by God's direction, smote the rock and God provided water in a miraculous way. Almost immediately after this, the Amalekites came against the Israelites to make war with them, the first battle the Israelites had to fight during their days of march.

At this point Joshua is named for the first time: "And Moses said unto Joshua, Choose us out men, and go out, and fight with Amalek" (Ex. 17:9). So we first meet Joshua as the general of the forces of the Lord, a role that would immediately in this setting teach him a lesson, namely, that God will not tolerate the rebellion of men against himself.

The Amalekites, of course, were not a part of the promise made to Abraham. They were non-Jews—Semitic, but non-Jews. Here the Amalekites were, rebelling against the living God. This action is clearly portrayed as rebellion in Exodus 17:16: "Because the hand of Amalek is against the throne of the Lord [or, Because there is a hand against the throne of Jehovah], therefore hath the LORD sworn, the LORD will have war with Amalek from generation to generation." In other words, the war of Amalek and the Amalekites against the Israelites was not just the surrounding world making war with God's people; the war was a blow against the throne of God. The Amalekites were challenging with the sword God's rule, God's throne, God's rightful place over all the world.

Exodus 17:16 indicates that the Amalekites understood something of the fact that they were fighting not only against the Israelites but also against the God who stood behind the Israelites. One can question how much knowledge they had, but their actions remind me of twentieth-century men who understand that what they are really fighting against is at least the concept of the Judeo-Christian religion and the culture which was based upon it.

So Joshua is introduced to us as a general in the midst of a warfare which impressed upon him that God will not tolerate the rebellion of men against himself.

Joshua also learned another important lesson through the conflict with the Amalekites: Power is not merely the power of the general and the sword, but power is the power of God. Moses sent Joshua out to fight while he himself climbed to the top of a hill with the rod of God in his hand—the same rod that he had stretched over the Red Sea till it had rolled back, the same rod that God had used in many of the miracles. The rod had originally been the rod of Moses but had become the rod of God, a representation of God's power. As the rod was raised, the Israelites prevailed; as it sank, the Amalekites prevailed (Ex. 17:11). This is not to be thought of as magic. God was teaching these people a serious lesson in their first warfare, and no one was to learn it better than Joshua the general. In the midst of battle, is one to fight? Yes. To be a good general? Yes. But when everything is done, the power is to be understood as God's not man's.

In Exodus 17:14 another note is added: "And the LORD said unto Moses, Write this for a memorial in *the* book. . . ." It seems clear that a definite article is used here. There was a book of God which continued to grow, and this was the Pentateuch itself. What was written in it was what God said should be put there. Early in Joshua's life, therefore, he was in a definite way wrapped up with *the book*. As we shall see, this becomes exceedingly important in the book of Joshua itself.

On Mount Sinai

The next time we see Joshua is in Exodus 24:13: "And Moses rose up, and his minister Joshua: And Moses went up into the mount of God." Immediately before this, these two men had been joined by some others for a very special event: "Then up went Moses, and Aaron, Nadab, and Abihu, and seventy of the elders of Israel: And they saw the God of Israel: and there was under his feet as it were a paved work of a sapphire stone, and as it were the very heaven for clearness. And upon the nobles of the children of Israel he laid not his hand: also they saw God, and did eat and drink" (Ex. 24:9-11).

The leaders went part way up the mount, and they ate. Then Joshua apparently went up still further with Moses. In this event were two strong emphases: the first upon *the reality of God* and the second on *the glory of God*. All the leaders would have perceived this as they ate before him.

The eating before God was not unique. In fact, one of

11

the great things in Scripture is that we eat before God. This is beautiful, because eating is such a lowly activity. It is connected with our body and our bodily functions in a way that hardly anything else is, for what we eat becomes our body. Yet constantly in the Scriptures God's people are brought together to eat in his presence. For instance, the Passover, which was established at Mount Sinai, was really an eating in the presence of God. So is the Lord's Supper, which took place in the New Testament and continues today. Finally, we are expressly told that at the second coming the marriage supper of the Lamb will take place and all the redeemed in resurrection bodies will eat in the presence of God. Among the many things which are marvelous about this is the very reality of it—the solidness of it. It highlights the fact that the whole man was made by God and is accepted by God.

Another thing is clearly seen in God's preparation of Joshua: Joshua was reminded of the interplay between the seen and the unseen worlds. There is no vast chasm between them; the unseen world is right here. The unseen world is always immediately present, not far off. Above everything and overshadowing everything is the reality of God in his glory. It undoubtedly stood Joshua in good stead many times in the future for him to understand that God was close at hand, that he is the God who exists and who is "here."

In Exodus 24:17 we read, "And the sight of the glory of the LORD was like devouring fire on the top of the mount in the eyes of the children of Israel." All the children of Israel saw space-time, historic manifestations on the top of Mount Sinai, so that later, after this generation had died, Moses could stand on the plain of Moab and say to those who had been little children when these manifestations occurred, "You saw! You heard!" This is the very opposite of the modern concept of the existential religious leap, for it is woven into a strong space-time fabric.

At the Golden Calf

Joshua is mentioned next at a very sober time, the time of the golden calf (Ex. 32). God said to Moses, "Go down quickly, because even while you've been up here on the mount, the people have revolted against me!" So down came Moses and Joshua from the mountain.

As he came down, "Joshua heard the noise of the people as they shouted, [and] he said unto Moses, There is a noise of war in the camp" (Ex. 32:17). Maybe he heard this with his general's ears, with his mind attuned to battle. But Moses responded, "It has nothing to do with war." It would have been much better if it had been war, for it was something much more serious. "It is not the voice of them that shout for mastery," Moses said. "Neither is it the voice of them that cry for being overcome: but the noise of them that sing do I hear" (v. 18). "Singing," you say. "Well, that's better than war." In this case, though, it was worse. War is not the greatest evil to come upon a people. "And it came to pass, as soon as he came nigh unto the camp, that he saw the calf, and the dancing: and Moses' anger waxed hot, and he cast the tables out of his hands, and brake them beneath [at the foot of] the mount" (v. 19).

Let us visualize Moses' response. He came down from the mountain and into the foothills—the slope at the bottom. He and Joshua saw the golden calf, and Moses immediately smashed the tablets of stone upon which God had written the Ten Commandments. These were the very tablets upon which God himself had written with his finger. God had communicated in verbalized form and brought his words onto the tablets in the language of the people. Now Moses had destroyed them.

Imagine how the young man Joshua felt. Moses had left him and gone beyond. There had been thunder and lightning. Moses came down and had stone tablets in his hands, and on these tablets were words which could be read, words which had been placed there by God himself. Imagine the emotion! Yet, when the two men came back into the camp, the people were in total rebellion. Here Joshua learned another truth: the terribleness of sin, especially among the people of God. This was sobering, and Joshua never forgot it.

The people made a god that was no god. And, as soon as they had done this, there was a complete moral breakdown. The people took off their clothes and threw themselves into the same kind of sexual rite that was practiced by the cultures which surrounded them. We can think here of the orgy in Schönberg's opera, *Moses and Aaron*. Though most of the rest of the opera is not true to the Scriptures, this part is. There was an orgy at the golden calf. In this case the moral breakdown was not separated from their worship but was properly connected with it, because they were worshiping a god that was no god. As Paul points out in Romans 1, turning away from the living God always leads to moral breakdown. It has in our day. The last few generations have turned away from the living God, and now we are surrounded by a moral breakdown, including an all-prevailing sexual orgy.

In addition to having this terribleness impressed upon him, Joshua also saw that merely using the name of God is not sufficient. After Aaron had made the calf, he said, "This is thy god, O Israel, which brought thee up out of the land of Egypt" (Ex. 32:4). According to tradition, the children of Israel actually placed the most holy name of God— the Tetragrammaton—on the golden calf. But merely to use the name was nothing. This was worse, much worse, than not using the name of God at all. So Joshua would have understood that merely using the name of God is not enough.

Joshua would also have seen that there is a place for godly anger. Moses broke the tables and God never scolded him for this, not even a little. There was good reason for Moses' anger. After he had broken the tables of stone, Moses ground up the golden calf, put the powder upon the water and said to Israel, "All right! This is your drinking water. Go and drink it!"—a tremendous statement of godly anger against that which is sinful. We must say that the exercise of godly anger is dangerous to us because we so often mix it with egoism. But let us not forget that there *is* a place for godly anger. There were times when Christ, too, was angry. We can think, for example, of Christ driving out the money changers (John 2:15) and his being angry at the abnormality of death before the tomb of Lazarus (John 11:33).

In the Tabernacle

The fourth time we see Joshua is in Exodus 33: "And it came to pass, as Moses entered into the tabernacle, the cloudy pillar descended, and stood at the door of the tabernacle, and the LORD talked with Moses. . . . And the LORD spake unto Moses face to face, as a man speaketh unto his friend. And he turned again into the camp: but his servant Joshua, the son of Nun, a young man, departed not out of the tabernacle" (vv. 9, 11). Moses was unique: The Lord spoke with him face to face, as one speaks to his friend; and in the midst of this unusual situation, the young man Joshua was being taught; Joshua was going to school; Joshua was being prepared for his future leadership. It was imperative that he learn, since the great man Moses would die and Joshua would be left to carry on. Here, as in Exodus 24, he learned the reality of God in his glory, but with an additional note: God could and would guide. God not only exists but he guides his people as they live in, and walk through, the world of time and space.

Prophesying in the Camp

Joshua is next mentioned in an intriguing passage in Numbers:

And Moses went out, and told the people the words of

the LORD, and gathered the seventy men of the elders of the people, and set them round about the tabernacle. And the LORD came down in a cloud, and spake unto him, and took of the spirit that was upon him, and gave it unto the seventy elders: and it came to pass, that, when the spirit rested upon them, they prophesied, and did not cease. But there remained two of the men in the camp, the name of the one was Eldad, and the name of the other Medad: and the spirit rested upon them; and they were of them that were written, but went not out unto the tabernacle: and they prophesied in the camp. And there ran a young man, and told Moses, and said, Eldad and Medad do prophesy in the camp. And Joshua the son of Nun, the servant of Moses, one of his young men, answered and said, My lord Moses, forbid them. And Moses said unto him, Enviest thou for my sake? would God that all the LORD's people were prophets, and that the LORD would put his spirit upon them! (Num. 11:24-29)

Joshua had another lesson to learn, and a very serious one: God's glory is to come first. There is a great difference between leadership and self-aggrandizement. There is to be leadership among the people of God, according to the gifts he bestows, but there is not to be glorification of oneself or other men. Joshua asked that Eldad and Medad be forbidden to prophesy because they had not come before Moses in the tabernacle; but Moses answered magnificently, "Don't envy for my sake." Maybe Moses' response is one of the reasons the Bible says that Moses was a meek man. Though Moses was such a tremendous leader, he would not tolerate Joshua's glorifying him.

The young man Joshua was learning a lesson that anybody who is ever going to be worth anything in leadership must learn. None of us learns it completely, of course, and yet we must master it if we are going to be of any use in the church of God. A leader must never confuse himself with

God. When a person begins to exercise certain gifts and God brings him to a place of leadership in the church of Christ, how easy it is to do this. Yet this is the destruction of all true spiritual leadership.

Joshua also had to learn that a person cannot bind God with man-made rules. Joshua had a man-made rule: God really should not have placed his Spirit on the two men in the camp. This did not fit into Joshua's concept of what was good and proper. God has bound himself with rules based on his own character, which he will never break, but men (including God's leaders) must never try to bind him with their own rules. He will not keep these rules.

Spying Out the Land

In Numbers 13 we see more of Joshua's preparation. He was one of the twelve men God sent to spy out the promised land. The sixth verse says that from the tribe of Judah Caleb was sent, and the eighth verse mentions "of the tribe of Ephraim, Oshea, the son of Nun." In the sixteenth verse, we find that "Moses called Oshea the son of Nun Jehoshua." So this was Joshua. *Oshea* means "he saves," but Moses changed his name to *Jehoshua,* "Jehovah saves," so that Joshua would even in his name remember that it is not man who saves, but God who must save. *Jesus,* of course, is the Greek form for the Hebrew name *Joshua.*

When the spies returned, they gave contrasting opinions. The majority advised, "No. Trying to conquer the land is too dangerous. The people are too great." But two of the spies, Caleb and Joshua, remembered who God is and reported in line with the greatness of God and his covenant promises: "And Caleb stilled the people before Moses, and said, Let us go up at once, and possess it; for we are well able to overcome it" (Num. 13:30). Here Caleb was affirming, "It's a great land, and we will be able to conquer it because we have a great God."

The people, however, followed the ten spies. "All the

congregation lifted up their voice, and cried; and the people wept that night" (Num. 14:1). We can see the fiber of these two men as they spoke out and rebuked those who were following the majority report:

> And Joshua the son of Nun, and Caleb the son of Jephunneh, which were of them that searched the land, rent their clothes: And they spake unto all the company of the children of Israel, saying, The land, which we passed through to search it, is an exceeding good land. If the LORD delight in us, then he will bring us into this land, and give it us; a land which floweth with milk and honey. Only rebel not ye against the LORD, neither fear ye the people of the land; for they are bread for us: their defence is departed from them, and the LORD is with us: fear them not. (Num. 14:6-9)

Despite the rebuke, the people still acted upon the *majority report*. I emphasize this phrase for a purpose. We cannot go by majority reports. A democracy works on the basis of the majority, but this does not imply, by any means, that the majority opinion is always right. In this case, the majority was desperately wrong. Two against ten—nevertheless the minority was right! When the people acted upon the majority report, they were indeed doing what Joshua and Caleb warned them against—they were rebelling against God.

So the young man Joshua learned another lesson. He learned that, even when the majority was totally against him, he had to be willing to stand with God. He had to resist his own people when they were wrong, even if it led to physical danger. In this case it did: "But all the congregation bade stone them with stones" (Num. 14:10). "Kill these two! Get them out of the way!" the majority cried out. The people did not kill Joshua and Caleb; nevertheless, Joshua learned to exhibit courage even in the midst of physical danger and even though the majority in error were the people of God.

Joshua also learned once more the terribleness of rebel-

lion against God among God's own people, for God decreed
that none of these rebels would enter the promised land.
We must understand that this moment was a watershed.
Back around 2000 B.C. God had given a promise to Abraham, and the Jewish *race* had begun. Before that, there
were Semitic people, but no Jews. In the time of Moses
(about five hundred years later) that which had been a race
was constituted a *nation* when the people came out of Egypt,
crossed over the Red Sea, came to Sinai and received their
laws from God. The Bible was not only their religious law;
it was also their civil law as a nation. All that remained,
therefore, was to possess the land.

For the Jews the land was the cord which bound together
the other blessings. The Abrahamic covenant included a
national promise to the Jews which was related to the land.
The first promise God had given to Abraham was, "Get
thee out of thy country, and from thy kindred, and from
thy father's house, unto a land that I will shew thee" (Gen.
12:1). When God next spoke to Abraham, he emphasized
the same thing: "For all the land which thou seest, to thee
will I give it, and to thy seed forever.... Arise, walk
through the land in the length of it and in the breadth of it;
for I will give it unto thee" (Gen. 13:15, 17). Later, God said
to Abraham, "I am the LORD that brought thee out of Ur
of the Chaldees, to give thee this land to inherit it" (Gen.
15:7).

But God also told Abraham he would not have the land
at once: "Know of a surety that thy seed shall be a stranger
in a land that is not their's, and shall serve them; and they
shall afflict them four hundred years; ... but in the fourth
generation they shall come hither again: for the iniquity of
the Amorites is not yet full" (Gen. 15:13, 16). God told
Abraham that his descendants were not going to have the
land immediately and that there was a reason for this: The
iniquity of the Amorites was not yet full.

At the time the spies went out, the iniquity of the Amorites had become full, so it was time to go into the land. The third piece was now to be put into place: The race, the nation and the land were to be brought together.

The Israelites had traveled from Egypt to Sinai in only two months. God kept them at Sinai for one year, to consolidate them, no doubt, and especially to give them the Ten Commandments, the entire civil law and all the other great things that are revealed in the books of Moses. This means that by the time the spies went out, only one year and two months had elapsed from the people's being slaves in Egypt to the complex of the race, the nation and the land standing ready to be fulfilled. Suddenly came the rebellion of the people, and God stretched out a year and two months into forty years. For thirty-eight years after this, the Israelites wandered in the wilderness until everybody over the age of twenty, except Joshua and Caleb had died.

So Joshua learned a lesson of the terribleness, even in the present life, of God's people rebelling against him. Surely, he never forgot—thirty-eight years lost because of rebellion! Rebellion against God is no light thing. It always brings its results in the present life. At this time it postponed the completion of the complex of race, nation and land.

God told the people, "Doubtless ye shall not come into the land, concerning which I sware to make you dwell therein, save Caleb the son of Jephunneh and Joshua the son of Nun" (Num. 14:30). Only two people who were adults at this time would live to go in. Here Joshua learned something else: God keeps his promises. Just imagine the Israelites as they walked for thirty-eight years through the wilderness. One person would die, and then another; one set of bones would be laid aside, and then another, until every single person was dead. Moses went into the plain of Moab with only two men from that generation behind him —Joshua and Caleb. Joshua saw in dramatic fashion that God keeps his promises and distinguishes among men in the structure of history.

Joshua's Ordination

On the plain of Moab, when "there was not left a man of them, save Caleb the son of Jephunneh, and Joshua the son of Nun" (Num. 26:65), the time came for Joshua's ordination. This is what we read:

And the LORD said unto Moses, Take thee Joshua the son of Nun, a man in whom is the spirit, and lay thine hand upon him; and set him before Eleazar the priest, and before all the congregation; and give him a charge in their sight. And thou shalt put some of thine honour upon him, that all the congregation of the children of Israel may be obedient. And he shall stand before Eleazar the priest, who shall ask counsel for him after the judgment of Urim before the LORD: at his word shall they go out, and at his word they shall come in, both he, and all the children of Israel with him, even all the congregation. And Moses did as the LORD commanded him: and he took Joshua, and set him before Eleazar the priest, and before all the congregation: And he laid his hands upon him, and gave him a charge, as the LORD commanded by the hand of Moses. (Num. 27:18-23)

After all the years of preparation, Joshua was now marked, in the presence of God's people, as the man of God's choice. Thus he would have learned that leadership, if it is real, is not from men. It was not even from Moses, but only from God. Men can ordain, but leadership does not derive from them. Men, even Christian men, can generate leadership, but leadership generated only by men is only on the level of any human leadership and will bring no more true spiritual results than any human charisma.

Moses' Final Address

In the book of Deuteronomy, we are close to the end of the time of Moses and close to the beginning of the book of Joshua. Moses addressed the people several times before his death, and among his words were these:

I am an hundred and twenty years old this day; I can no more go out and come in: also the LORD hath said unto me, Thou shalt not go over this Jordan. The LORD thy God, he will go over before thee, and he will destroy these nations from before thee, and thou shalt possess them: and Joshua, he shall go over before thee, as the LORD hath said. And the LORD shall do unto them as he did to Sihon and to Og, kings of the Amorites, and unto the land of them whom he destroyed. And the LORD shall give them up before your face, that ye may do unto them according unto all the commandments which I have commanded you. Be strong and of a good courage, fear not, nor be afraid of them: for the LORD thy God, he it is that doth go with thee; he will not fail thee, nor forsake thee. And Moses called unto Joshua, and said unto him in the sight of all Israel, Be strong and of a good courage: for thou must go with this people unto the land which the LORD hath sworn unto their fathers to give them; and thou shalt cause them to inherit it. And the LORD, he it is that doth go before thee; he will be with thee, he will not fail thee, neither forsake thee: fear not, neither be dismayed. (Deut. 31:2-8)

"I am going to die," Moses said, "but don't be afraid. God is going to go over before you." Notice the order, which must not get reversed. God goes before; therefore, his people can go without fear. The human leader, Joshua, went before, too, but the reason Joshua could go without fear was not that his natural abilities and his faithfulness were so great (though these were evident by this time) but that God would go before him. This order must always be carefully maintained.

Undoubtedly Moses was thinking back to the time thirty-eight years before when the parents of these people were afraid and God condemned them to die in the wilderness;

so he warned, "Don't do it again!" But there was something else. Moses was pointing out that as God had acted in the past he would act in the future. The promises were not "pie in the sky."

Those who are the people of God should reflect often on the continuity of the promises of God. The people of God should look back through the Scripture. They should also be able to look back through the history of their own lives. Seeing that God has cared for them in the past, they should not be afraid of tomorrow, because God is going to go before them then as well. Moses' tremendous emphasis was that the reason the people did not need to be afraid was not that they had Joshua (though wasn't it wonderful that they did have Joshua?) but that God would go before both them and Joshua.

So we see here three steps: The Lord goes before his people, the Lord goes before the human leader and then the people can go without fear. The line is laid down. And as it has been in the past it will be in the future.

Shortly after Moses spoke these words, a touching thing occurred—touching because it hearkened back to a memory from Joshua's youth. Now, when Joshua was much older, "The LORD said unto Moses, Behold, thy days approach that thou must die: call Joshua, and present yourselves in the tabernacle of the congregation, that I may give him a charge. And Moses and Joshua went, and presented themselves in the tabernacle of the congregation. And the LORD appeared in the tabernacle in a pillar of a cloud: and the pillar of the cloud stood over the door of the tabernacle" (Deut. 31:14-15). We do not know if this had happened many times in the intervening years, but we do know that when Joshua was a young man he had gone into the tabernacle with Moses, and the cloud of the glory of God had come down upon them. I think God means for us to see a link. As a young man, Joshua had learned something. As the time came for Joshua to step out into leadership, this lesson was repeated. The two men were again in the tabernacle, directly under the Shekinah glory of God.

In Deuteronomy 31 is another point of extreme importance. "Moses went and spake these words unto all Israel," verse 1 tells us. This was a verbalized communication from God through Moses. But in verses 9-12 the importance of this is brought to its peak:

And Moses wrote this law, and delivered it unto the priests the sons of Levi, which bare the ark of the covenant of the LORD, and unto all the elders of Israel. And Moses commanded them, saying, At the end of every seven years, in the solemnity of the year of release, in the feast of tabernacles, when all Israel is come to appear before the LORD thy God in the place which he shall choose, thou shalt read this law before all Israel in their hearing. Gather the people together, men, and women, and children, and thy stranger that is within thy gates, that they may hear, and that they may learn, and fear the LORD your God, and observe to do all the words of this law.

The commands of God were carried through Moses to the people in a written, propositional form. We are watching here the Scripture growing before our eyes. The text has already said that Moses wrote; now he writes again. And what is he writing? The Pentateuch—Genesis, Exodus, Leviticus, Numbers and Deuteronomy.

In verses 24-26 the mention of the Pentateuch continues:

And it came to pass, when Moses had made an end of writing the words of this law in a book, until they were finished, that Moses commanded the Levites, which bare the ark of the covenant of the LORD, saying, Take this book of the law, and put it in the side of the ark of the covenant of the LORD your God, that it may be there for a witness against thee.

The book was placed in the ark or by the ark to remind the people that it was connected with God. It was the Word of

God in written form. The first five books of the Bible were now complete. God had given in written propositional form the great religious truths he wanted men to have up till that point of history, and he had told them, and us, facts of the cosmos and history as well.

Deuteronomy 34:7-8 describes the death of Moses: "And Moses was an hundred and twenty years old when he died: his eye was not dim, nor his natural force abated. And the children of Israel wept for Moses in the plains of Moab thirty days: so the days of weeping and mourning for Moses were ended." Joshua, I think, learned his final lesson in preparation: No man is indispensable. I do not like that statement if it is left alone, simply because I think the Bible says more than that. We must say, "No man is indispensable," but we must not forget Deuteronomy 34:10: "And there arose not a prophet since in Israel like unto Moses, whom the LORD knew face to face." Here Moses' uniqueness is emphasized. So we can say at the same time, without being contradictory: No man is indispensable, but every man is unique. Men are dispensable; but this does not mean that one man fills another man's place in the same way as a person would remove one concrete block and put another concrete block in its place. In the final analysis, nobody takes the place of anybody else. This is the wonder of personality and the wonder of God using personality in leadership.

Joshua Is Ready

Now, after all these years of preparation, Joshua was ready to enter the land: "And Joshua the son of Nun was full of the spirit of wisdom; for Moses had laid his hands upon him: and the children of Israel hearkened unto him, and did as the LORD commanded Moses" (Deut. 34:9). This was not a mechanical readiness. An act of the will was involved. If we do not stress this, we will be giving an inaccurate picture of Joshua's preparation. It is not that you feed preparation into a mill and a leader comes out the other end. It is not that way, any more than that you feed facts into a mill and a Christian comes out the other end. There must be an act of the will in becoming a Christian, and there must be an act of the will for any man, no matter what his preparation, to become a leader in God's work.

At the end of his own life, Joshua said to the people, "And if it seem evil unto you to serve the LORD, choose you this day whom ye will serve; whether the gods which your fathers served that were on the other side of the flood, or the gods of the Amorites in whose land ye dwell: but as for me and my house, we will serve the LORD" (Josh. 24:15). This was not a choice Joshua made only at the end of his life. All through his preparation we see a series of acts of his will.

There is no leader who does not have to choose. You can take two men with equal preparation, and one serves the Lord while the other does not. We must realize that whether we are young or old God does not deal with us as sticks and stones. He has made us as people, and he expects us to respond as people. Even when God has prepared a person, if there is to be real spiritual leadership, the leadership will require a constant, existential, moment-by-moment act of the will: "If the rest of you wish to go the way of the majority, go! As for me and my house, we will serve the Lord."

Is there always a long time of preparation for spiritual leadership? Not always, but usually. We can think of those in the Scripture, including Christ, who for years were prepared for the crucial leadership they would exercise. We must be careful; we cannot make this a rule, because Paul did say to Timothy, "Let no man despise thy youth" (1 Tim. 4:12). We must not insist that no man can be given important leadership until he has gray hair—or no hair at all! At the same time, we must understand that if we are young and want to be used in the Lord's work we must be ready for a time of preparation. Usually there is preparation before leadership. Both Moses and Joshua had many, many years of preparation.

Let us review what Joshua learned in his preparation: God will not tolerate the rebellion of men against himself.

Power is not merely the power of the general and the sword. It is not to be the power of man, but true power is the power of God.

God is not far off; God is always immediately present.

Sin is terrible, especially among the people of God.

Merely using the name of God is not sufficient.

God can and will guide.

God's glory is to come first. There is a real difference between leadership and self-aggrandizement.

A person cannot bind God with man-made rules.

A man of God must stand and trust God—even against his own people, even if in the minority, even in the midst of physical danger.

Even in his judgment, God keeps his promises and distinguishes among men. He does not treat men like a series of numbers.

True spiritual leadership does not come from the hands of men but from God.

No man is indispensable, yet each man is important and unique.

Usually there is preparation before leadership.

God taught Joshua all these things as Joshua followed Moses in the wilderness. Then, with these lessons learned, Joshua was ready to lead the people into the promised land.

two
The Three Changeless Factors

After Joshua acted as the general against the Amalekites, "the LORD said unto Moses, Write this for a memorial in a book" (Ex. 17:14). This book became the center of the life of the people of Israel from this point on. Over and over the Pentateuch tells how it came to be composed. In Numbers, for example, we find, "And Moses wrote their goings out according to their journeys by the commandment of the LORD" (Num. 33:2). Just as Exodus 17 specifically refers to the writing of the book of Exodus, Numbers 33 specifically refers to the writing of the book of Numbers.

In the plain of Moab, with the forty-year wandering over, the writing still continued under the command of God. Deuteronomy 31 portrays the growth of the Pentateuch, emphasizing that Moses wrote in the book. Of course, one of the liberal theories is that the Pentateuch was carried down through the spoken word for a long period prior to the writing. But this theory directly contradicts what the Pentateuch itself claims, because in Deuteronomy 31:9 we read, "And Moses wrote this law, and delivered it unto the priests the sons of Levi." So Moses not only spoke; he also wrote. He gave propositional verbalized communication from God to man in written as well as spoken form. We are told about the production of Exodus, Numbers and Deuteronomy. Something was *written.*

Deuteronomy 31 also makes clear that what was written was not to be a priestly book, hidden away from the people, as if they could not understand it. Quite the contrary—from time to time it was to be read not only before the priests but also before the common people:

And Moses wrote this law, and delivered it unto the priests the sons of Levi, which bare the ark of the covenant of the LORD, and unto all the elders of Israel. And Moses commanded them, saying, At the end of every seven years, in the solemnity of the year of release, in the feast of tabernacles, when all Israel is come to appear before the LORD thy God in the place which he shall choose, thou shalt read this law before all Israel in their hearing. Gather the people together, men, and women, and children, and thy stranger that is within thy gates, that they may hear, and that they may learn, and fear the LORD your God, and observe to do all the words of this law: and that their children, which have not known any thing, may hear, and learn to fear the LORD your God, as long as ye live in the land whither ye go over Jordan to possess it. (Deut. 31:9-13)

The people, of course, could not have their own Bibles. This would not be possible until after Gutenberg. But this does not mean that the Pentateuch was an exotic book, a mere symbol. It was not like the ark of the Lord, never to be seen. While the ark of the Lord was hidden away from the common eyes and covered when the people traveled, the book was brought out periodically and read. This was a reminder, therefore, that it was not a book too holy for common use. It was important because it was from God, but it was common because it was to be understood by all the people. The people were to know the content which God had given through Moses in the book.

In Deuteronomy 31:19 Moses speaks of "this song." One of the liberal theories is that the Pentateuch was passed down by song and only written down much later, but again the book of Deuteronomy contradicts this. While it is true that the people were to learn the song and pass it on to their children, the text also says, "Write ye this song."

We see, then, a sequential structure: God commanded something to be written in a book, and Moses wrote it over a period of forty years. As we get to the end of the book of Deuteronomy, the writing of Moses is finished. When Moses completed the Pentateuch, he commanded that it be kept in a sacred place, "in the side of the ark of the covenant" (Deut. 31:26). It was to be preserved and read regularly to all the people.

The First Changeless Factor: The Written Book

This brings us, finally, to Joshua 1:

Now after the death of Moses the servant of the LORD it came to pass, that the LORD spake unto Joshua the son of Nun, Moses' minister, saying, Moses my servant is dead; now therefore arise, go over this Jordan, thou, and all this people, unto the land which I do give to them, even to the children of Israel. Every place that the sole of your foot shall tread upon, that have I given unto you, as I said unto Moses. From the wilderness and this Lebanon even unto the great river, the river Euphrates, all the land of the Hittites, and unto the great sea toward the going down of the sun, shall be your coast. There shall not any man be able to stand before thee all the days of thy life: as I was with Moses, so I will be with thee: I will not fail thee, nor forsake thee. Be strong and of a good courage: for unto this people shalt thou divide for an inheritance the land, which I sware unto their fathers to give them. Only be thou strong and very courageous, that thou mayest observe to do according to all the law, which Moses my servant commanded thee: turn not from it to the right hand or to the left, that thou mayest prosper whithersoever thou goest. This book of the law shall not depart out of thy mouth; but thou shalt meditate therein day and night, that thou mayest observe to do according to all that is written therein: for then thou shalt make thy way prosperous, and then thou shalt have good success [or, do wisely]. (Josh. 1:1-8)

As the Israelites stood ready to enter the land, God's main emphasis was upon *the book.*

Joshua was to have special revelations from God through the priest: "And he [Joshua] shall stand before Eleazar the priest, who shall ask counsel of him after the judgment of Urim before the LORD" (Num. 27:21). We are not sure exactly what the Urim was, the way it functioned or how God used it to reveal himself, but we do know it was one way God, through the priest, revealed propositional content to his people. But though Joshua was going to have this special leading from the Lord, this was not to detract from the central reference point and chief control: the written book. The Word of God written in the book set the limitations. Thus, Joshua was already functioning in the way Bible-believing Christians function. Sometimes God does lead in other ways, but such leading must always be within the circle of his external, propositional commands in Scripture. Even if a person had an Urim and a Thummim as well as a priest to guide him, this would not change his basic authority. The primary leading would come from the written, propositional revelation of God, from the Bible.

So we see that the written book was the first of the three changeless factors that stood with Joshua as he assumed leadership. "Only be thou strong and very courageous," God commanded him, "that thou mayest observe to do according to all the law, which Moses my servant commanded thee: turn not from it to the right hand or to the left, that thou mayest prosper whithersoever thou goest. This book of the law shall not depart out of thy mouth; but thou shalt meditate therein day and night, that thou mayest observe to do according to all that is written therein: for then thou shalt make thy way prosperous, and then thou shalt have good success [or, do wisely]." Joshua had been walking beside Moses (the young man beside the older) for forty years, yet God's command to Joshua was not just general. It was not, "Try to remember what Moses told you and follow it." Rather, Joshua was to search out and constantly study the sharp and definite commands in the written book.

The Lord especially emphasized three things. First, the law was not to depart out of Joshua's mouth; he was to talk about it. Second, he was to meditate on it day and night. Meditation is a cognitive activity; it takes place in the area of reason. God's law is not something that should be mechanically reproduced, nor is it contentless (to express it in contemporary terms).

Third, he was to practice the commands in his historic, space-time situation. Talk about it; think about it; do it! Jesus' teaching had the same emphasis, "Here are my words. Do them!"

Throughout his life, Joshua was obedient. Of all the factors which gave him such success the most important was that he heeded God's admonition about the book. For example, at Ebal and Gerizim Joshua carried out exactly Moses' instruction to read the law before all the people. (See Josh. 8; we will study this in more detail in chapter 7.) Joshua lived out his life in a practical way within the circle of the written revelation.

This faithfulness continued to the end of his life. Joshua's charge to the people when he was ready to die was simple and final: "Be ye therefore very courageous to keep and to do all that is written in the book of the law of Moses, that ye turn not aside therefrom to the right hand or to the left" (Josh. 23:6). Joshua kept the command of God all the days of his life, and, before he died, he urged the people that followed him to do the same: "Live your life within the circle of the propositions given in the written book."

The Growth and Acceptance of the Canon

Joshua's relation to the book teaches us an important lesson about how the canon grew and was accepted. Joshua knew Moses, the writer of the Pentateuch, personally. Joshua knew his strengths and weaknesses as a man; he knew that Moses was a sinner, that Moses made mistakes, that Moses was just a man. Nonetheless, immediately after Moses' death Joshua accepted the Pentateuch as more than the writing of Moses. He accepted it as the writing of God. Two or three hundred years were not required for the book to become sacred. As far as Joshua was concerned the Pentateuch was the canon, and the canon was the Word of God. The biblical view of the growth and acceptance of the canon is as simple as this: When it was given, God's people understood what it was. Right away it had authority.

This is why I think the book of Joshua is so crucial. It stands as the bridge between the Pentateuch and the post-Pentateuchal period and provides the key for understanding some important relationships between various parts of the whole Scripture.

The fact that Joshua's generation accepted the Pentateuch as authoritative is more than a mere breath of fresh air in the heavy smog which surrounds present liberal scholarly discussion. To the Israelites, the canon was not just academic, not merely theological, but practical. Joshua and the people had a continuity of authority as they moved through history. The book was to be their environment, their mentality.

At the time of Moses, they had the authority of both Moses and the law God had commanded Moses to write. When they woke up the morning after Moses died and when they entered the promised land, they were not left in a vacuum. To use another image, because of the continuity provided by the book, there was no fracture in the authority. In the practical problems of life, they had an objective standard of judgment which stood in an unbroken flow.

One practical problem, for instance, was how to judge prophecies. Moses had written that if a man made a prophecy and it did not come to pass it was not from God (Deut. 18:22). But this, of course, left an even more acute problem: What happens when people make strange prophecies that do come to pass? Then where do the prophecies come from? How can you tell? Moses had laid down these guidelines:

> What thing soever I command you, observe to do it: thou shalt not add thereto, nor diminish from it. If there arise among you a prophet, or a dreamer of dreams, and giveth thee a sign or a wonder, and the sign or the wonder come to pass, whereof he spake unto thee, saying, Let us go after other gods, which thou hast not known, and let us serve them; thou shalt not hearken unto the words of that prophet, or that dreamer of dreams: for the LORD your God proveth you, to know whether ye love the LORD your God with all your heart and with all your soul. Ye shall walk after the LORD your God, and fear him, and keep his commandments, and obey his voice, and ye shall serve him, and cleave unto him. And that prophet, or that dreamer of dreams, shall be put to death; because he hath spoken to turn you away from the LORD your God, which brought you out of the land of Egypt, and redeemed you out of the house of bondage, to thrust thee out of the way which the LORD thy God commanded thee to walk in. So shalt thou put the evil away from the midst of thee. (Deut. 12:32—13:5)

This passage from Deuteronomy reveals the standard that

God himself gave: Judge the prophet whose prophecy comes to pass by comparing what he says with the objective written standard. Whether a prophecy comes to pass or not is not the final test. The final test is whether a prophet's teaching stands in continuity with what is written in the book.

Because of the book, the first of the great changeless factors, God's people had a way to make objective, not merely experiential, judgments. The whole man, with his reason, could consider what Moses' writings said. In this time of change from the great lawgiver, Moses, to the post-Pentateuchal period, the Israelites had a standard, a very practical guide.

In the book of Joshua, we watch the canon grow even more. Joshua 5:1 contains the phrase *until we were passed over.* The person who wrote the narrative was there! (This reminds us of the "we" passages in Acts.) Joshua 5:6 has the words *which the LORD sware unto their fathers that he would give us, a land that floweth with milk and honey.* Again, the writer was present at these events. When the Pentateuch was finished, the book of Joshua, a continuation of the canon, flowed on; and it was a first-person situation.

Joshua 24:26 tells us who this person was: "And Joshua wrote these words in the book of the law." How did the canon grow? Moses wrote, and Moses died. Joshua continued to write, and the canon continued to grow. Incidentally, as a quick parenthesis, it is quite clear that the Bible always accepts Joshua as a historic character. Nehemiah 8:17 illustrates this when it says that the children of Israel had not kept the feast of booths since the days of Joshua the son of Nun.

As Joshua faced his task, then, he had with him this first great changeless factor: the written book. It provided a continuity of authority, but it was growing and would continue to grow. It grew, but it was not discontinuous. Joshua, as he led the people, had an objective standard by which to judge everything else, and the standard was so clear that God expected the ordinary people to understand it when it was periodically read to them.

The Second Changeless Factor: The Power of God
When the people were ready to enter the land, they left Shittim, an area on the east bank of the Jordan, where they had been lodging, and moved up to the east bank of the Jordan River. Three days later occurred an incident which revealed the second changeless factor: the power of God.

And the LORD said unto Joshua, This day will I begin to magnify thee in the sight of all Israel, that they may know that, as I was with Moses, so I will be with thee. And thou shalt command the priests that bear the ark of the covenant, saying, When ye are come to the brink of the water of Jordan, ye shall stand still in Jordan. And Joshua said unto the children of Israel, Come hither, and hear the words of the LORD your God. And Joshua said, Hereby ye shall know that the living God is among you, and that he will without fail drive out from before you the Canaanites, and the Hittites, and the Hivites, and the Perizzites, and the Girgashites, and the Amorites, and the Jebusites. Behold, the ark of the covenant of the LORD of all the earth passeth over before you into Jordan. Now therefore take you twelve men out of the tribes of Israel, out of every tribe a man. And it shall come to pass, as soon as the soles of the feet of the priests that bear the ark of the LORD, the Lord of all the earth, shall rest in the waters of Jordan, that the waters of Jordan shall be cut off from the waters that come down from above; and they shall stand upon an heap.

And it came to pass, when the people removed from their tents, to pass over Jordan, and the priests bearing the ark of the covenant before the people; and as they that bare the ark were come unto Jordan, and the feet of the priests that bare the ark were dipped in the brim of the water, (for Jordan overfloweth all his banks all the time of harvest,) that the waters which came down from above stood and rose up upon an heap very far from the city Adam, that is beside Zaretan: and those that came down toward the sea of the plain, even the salt sea, failed, and were cut off: and the people passed over right against Jericho. And the priests that bare the ark of the covenant of the LORD stood firm on dry ground in the midst of Jordan, and all the Israelites passed over on dry ground, until all the people were passed clean over Jordan. . . .

And it came to pass, when the priests that bare the ark of the covenant of the LORD were come up out of the midst of Jordan, and the soles of the priests' feet were lifted up unto the dry land, that the waters of Jordan returned unto their place, and flowed over all his banks, as they did before. (Josh. 3:7-17; 4:18)

The priests carried the ark into the Jordan, and, while they stood in the water, God rolled back the Jordan. How God did this we are not told. Whether it was by direct command or through some material means, as when the east wind blew back the Red Sea, does not matter. What matters is that the waters were stopped, even though it was the time of flood, and all the people passed over on dry land. Then the priests walked out and the waters returned.

God did a remarkable thing here, and the text expressly says that he did it for a purpose: "On that day the LORD magnified Joshua in the sight of all Israel; and they feared him, as they feared Moses, all the days of his life" (Josh. 4:14). God rolled back the waters for Joshua just as he had done for Moses forty years earlier. The exact sign he had given at the exodus from Egypt, he now gave at their entrance into the promised land. The sign which had most conclusively shown the power of God upon Moses was now associated with Joshua. "As I was with Moses, so I will be with thee," God had told Joshua (Josh. 3:7). Now he dramatically demonstrated that this was so.

The accounts of the two miracles even share some words in common. Joshua 3:13 and 3:16 speak of the waters standing "upon an heap." The song of Moses, in Exodus 15, states in poetic form that "the floods stood upright as an heap" (v. 8). God told Joshua to command the priests, "Ye shall stand still in Jordan" (Josh. 3:8). On the edge of the Red Sea, Moses said to the people, "Fear ye not, stand still, and see the salvation of the LORD (Ex. 14:13). These repetitions imply the parallel which the book of Joshua identifies explicitly: "For the LORD your God dried up the waters of Jordan from before you, until ye were passed over, as the LORD your God did to the Red sea" (Josh. 4:23).

To us, the parting of the Red Sea is ancient history, but to the people who watched the Jordan roll back, it was not. Joshua, Caleb and all the older people had been at the Red Sea, because those who were under twenty when the Red Sea was rolled back were still living. Therefore they were recalling something in their own personal history. We can picture these Israelites coming up to the River Jordan, the older ones remembering the Red Sea, and the younger ones recalling the accounts of their parents who over and over again had described to them the wonder of that event. Joshua and Caleb, especially, would have remembered. Then to have God suddenly give the same sign as they were entering the promised land—a symbol of the continuity of the authority and the power of God—must have given them a tremendous sense of wonder, awe and certainty.

Even at the end of his life, Joshua reminded the people that some of them could remember all that had happened in the days of Moses: "He put darkness between you and the Egyptians, and brought the sea upon them, and covered them; and your eyes have seen what I have done in Egypt. ... [God] did those great signs in our sight" (Josh. 24:7, 17). He was calling upon the older men and women to remember a history which was not just a history of the past (as it is to us), but a personal experience.

Joshua himself had also seen this power manifested in the battle against the Amalekites. When Moses had stood with his hands upheld, the Israelites had won; when his hands went down, the Amalekites had won. God certainly taught Joshua something to remember all the days of his life: "The power is mine! The power is mine!" As the people crossed over the Jordan, Joshua would have known again that the power was there and that it was a changeless power, not a power just for one period in history. The power was there, and the power was the Lord's. The power is not in anything or anybody independent of God. It is the same power through the whole Bible, and God's power is not diminished in our period of history. It is the same power: past, present and future.

The Third Changeless Factor: The Supernatural Leader

The third changeless factor is the continuity of a Person:

And it came to pass, when Joshua was by Jericho, that he lifted up his eyes and looked, and, behold, there stood a man over against him with his sword drawn in his hand: and Joshua went unto him, and said unto him, Art thou for us, or for our adversaries? And he said, Nay; but as captain of the host of the LORD am I now come. And Joshua fell on his face to the earth, and did worship, and said unto him, What saith my lord unto his servant? And the captain of the LORD's host said unto Joshua, Loose thy shoe from off thy foot; for the place whereon thou standest is holy. And Joshua did so. . . . And the LORD said unto Joshua, See, I have given into thine hand Jericho, and the king thereof, and the mighty men of valour. (Josh. 5:13-17; 6:2)

The power which continued in Joshua's time was neither impersonal nor magical. The power was related to a Person —a Person who also has continuity in history.

The continuity of the supernatural leader was made explicit in the incident near Jericho. Here the One who confronted Joshua said, "As captain of the host of the LORD am I now come," thus implying that he had been present before in a different capacity. Joshua had seen and known this Person in the past, but now he was coming in a specific capacity, as the captain of the host of the Lord.

This, too, paralleled Moses' experience. Moses was in the desert when he received his special call at the burning bush. Suddenly he was confronted with a Person—the great "I Am"—who said to him, "Draw not nigh hither: put off thy shoes from off thy feet, for the place whereon thou standest is holy ground" (Ex. 3:5). The captain of the Lord's host gave Joshua the same instructions (Josh. 5:15). Joshua, filled with emotion, would have quickly undone his sandals and kicked them off, realizing he was now in Moses' place.

When God spoke to Moses from the burning bush, he constantly mentioned the past. In light of the insistence of the text, I can never understand how liberal theologians can try to maintain that this was a God new to the Israelites. This idea would seem impossible, because in Exodus 3:6 we read, "I am the God of thy father, the God of Abraham, the God of Isaac, and the God of Jacob. And Moses hid his face...." He was hiding his face before the same God who had appeared to Abraham five hundred years before. In Exodus 3:15 God reiterates, "Thus shalt thou say unto the children of Israel, The LORD God of your fathers, the God of Abraham, the God of Isaac, and the God of Jacob, hath sent me unto you." So there was this strong emphasis: "I am not a new God; there is a continuity in who I am and in my leadership." Verse 16 also speaks of "the LORD God of your fathers." When God turned Moses' rod into a snake, it was a sign to Pharaoh. It was a sign to the people of God that God would accomplish a purpose among them. What was this purpose? "That they [the children of Israel] may believe that the LORD God of their fathers, the God of Abraham, the God of Isaac, and the God of Jacob, hath appeared unto thee" (Ex. 4:5). The sign was to be a proof to the people that there was a continuity of supernatural leadership, back to the time of Abraham and before.

At the end of his life, on the plain of Moab, Moses spoke about this continuity:

> I am an hundred and twenty years old this day; I can no more go out and come in: also the LORD hath said unto me, Thou shalt not go over this Jordan. The LORD thy God, he will go over before thee, and he will destroy these nations from before thee, and thou shalt possess them: and Joshua, he shall go over before thee, as the LORD hath said. And the LORD shall do unto them as he did to Sihon and to Og, kings of the Amorites, and unto the land of them, whom he destroyed. And the LORD shall give them up before your face, that ye may do unto them according unto all the commandments which I have commanded you. Be strong and of a good courage, fear not, nor be afraid of them: for the LORD thy God, he it is that doth do with thee; he will not fail thee, nor forsake thee. And Moses called unto Joshua, and said unto him in the sight of all Israel, Be strong and of a good courage: for thou must go with this people unto the land which the LORD hath sworn unto their fathers to give them; and thou shalt cause them to inherit it. And the LORD, he it is that doth go before thee; he will be with thee, he will not fail thee, neither forsake thee: fear not, neither be dismayed. (Deut. 31:2-8)

We find here a double continuity. Moses said to the people, "Don't be afraid. The same God who dealt with Sihon and Og will deal with the men across the river." Then, turning to Joshua, he exclaimed, "The same God who has been with me will go before you, Joshua. Don't be afraid!" Joshua had seen the leading of the Lord in the cloud and the fire. He had been in the tabernacle when God had spoken to Moses.

So he already knew this One who met him near Jericho. So Joshua, looking back across Jordan, would have remembered all the wonders he had seen under the leadership of this same supernatural leader.

When Joshua first saw the captain of the host of the Lord, he reacted as a real man. Sword in hand, Joshua rushed up and challenged him. When the Person spoke to Joshua, Joshua suddenly understood who this was, and back into his memory flowed all I have just mentioned plus much more, surely, that is not recorded. It must have been an overwhelming moment for Joshua as he was picking up the reins of the leadership of God's people. This was now much more than a memory; it was a historical reality in the here and now. Here and now was the same supernatural leader, the same Person. Moses was dead, but the true leader would go on. Because this One said to Joshua, "I have given into thine hand Jericho" (Josh. 6:2), and because he knew this One kept his promises, Joshua was able to turn to his people before the walls of Jericho and say without any fear, "Shout; for the LORD hath given you the city" (Josh. 6:16). Why? Because the power was personal, and the Person was there.

The Three Changeless Factors Today

As he passed from the Pentateuchal period into the post-Pentateuchal period, Joshua knew the book, the supernatural power and the supernatural leader who was the living God. We are not living in the time of Joshua, but the New Testament says that these three great changeless factors are true for us as the children of God today. These continuities flow from the Pentateuch through the rest of the Old Testament into the New Testament and down through history to us.

Listen to Paul: "If any man think himself to be a prophet, or spiritual, let him acknowledge that the things that I write unto you are the commandments of the Lord" (1 Cor. 14:37). Does that sound familiar? Of course! It is exactly what Moses said. If somebody comes to us, how are we to judge what he says? Judge, says Paul, on the basis of what God has written in the book. There is no difference whatsoever in the objective standard. We have the same high possibility of objectivity, but now in a book that is enlarged. The continuity that Joshua had in his time of need, we have in our own needy generation.

Paul wrote something similar to the Thessalonians: "Therefore, brethren, stand fast, and hold the traditions which ye have been taught, whether by word, or our epistle" (2 Thess. 2:15). Here again is a parallel to Moses.

Perhaps the clearest New Testament statement of the continuity of authority was made by Peter. He reminded his readers that he had stood on the Mount of Transfiguration. What a great certainty—to have heard the voice from heaven and seen Jesus glorified! Nevertheless, Peter said, "Yes, but that was mine; and you won't have that because you weren't there. But there's something greater that we share in common." To quote directly from his letter, "We have also a more sure word of prophecy; whereunto ye do well that ye take heed, as unto a light that shineth in a dark place, until the day dawn, and the day star arise in your hearts: knowing this first, that no prophecy of the scripture is of any private interpretation. For the prophecy came not in old time by the will of man: but holy men of God spake as they were moved by the Holy Ghost" (2 Pet. 1:19-21). Peter was saying the same thing as Paul. We have a written revelation; we can judge by it, and its authority is final.

Peter also brought the Old Testament and New Testament together: "That ye may be mindful of the words which were spoken before by the holy prophets, and of the commandment of us the apostles of the Lord and Saviour" (2 Pet. 3:2). He specifically included the writings of Paul in the continuity of authority: "And account that the longsuffering of our Lord is salvation; even as our beloved brother Paul also according to the wisdom given unto him hath writ-

ten unto you; as also in all his epistles, speaking in them of
these things; in which are some things hard to be understood, which they that are unlearned and unstable wrest, as
they do also the other scriptures, unto their own destruction." (2 Pet. 3:15-16).

We today have the first of the three changeless factors—
a written, objective, propositional authority. As God said to
Israel, "What thing soever I command you, observe to do it:
thou shalt not add thereto, nor diminish from it" (Deut.
12:32), John affirmed at the end of the Bible, in the book
of Revelation, "For I testify unto every man that heareth
the words of the prophecy of this book, If any man shall
add unto these things, God shall add unto him the plagues
that are written in this book: and if any man shall take away
from the words of the book of this prophecy, God shall take
away his part out of the book of life, and out of the holy city,
and from the things which are written in this book" (Rev.
22:18-19). It is as though God is saying, "How can you miss
this? There is continuity of written objective authority all
the way from the Pentateuch through the New Testament."

Concerning the second changeless factor, consider a
statement of the resurrected Jesus: "All power is given unto
me in heaven and in earth" (Mt. 28:18). The same power
which was exhibited at the time of Moses and Joshua, Jesus
claimed was now given to him. Jesus connected this statement to the coming of the power of the Holy Spirit: "Ye
shall receive power, after that the Holy Spirit is come upon
you: and ye shall be witnesses unto me both in Jerusalem,
and in all Judea, and in Samaria, and unto the uttermost
part of the earth" (Acts 1:8). As God said to Joshua, "Remember the power? The Red Sea and Jordan rolled back!"
Jesus declared to his disciples, "Don't be afraid, for this entire age will receive power from the indwelling Holy Spirit."

The power which parted the Red Sea and the Jordan
flows on constantly. Facing a lost world—Jerusalem, Samaria, the ends of the earth—till Jesus comes, the church of

45

God has that power. The same power is available to the people of God—in the past, present and future.

The continuity of the third changeless factor, the supernatural, divine leader, comes to us with special force. In 1 Corinthians 10:4, Paul discusses the time when Moses struck the rock: "And [our fathers] did all drink the same spiritual drink: for they drank out of that spiritual Rock that followed them: and that Rock was Christ." The One who was in the wilderness and the One who stood before Joshua and said, "As captain of the host of the LORD am I now come," is the same Person we know after the incarnation as Jesus Christ.

This Person spoke about the continuity of his leadership when he told his followers, "Lo, I am with you alway, even unto the end of the world" (Mt. 28:20). The One who was with Moses at the rock and with Joshua at the beginning of the campaign against Jericho has promised, "Till I come again, I will be with you."

It is wonderful that the same leader is with us. Was the captain who went before Joshua in his battles some human leader? No. Must we struggle today in our own wisdom and puny strength? No, the power is there. The same leader is present, and the same leader will lead.

When Joshua saw this leader, he "fell on his face to the earth, and did worship, and said unto him, What sayeth my lord unto his servant? And the captain of the LORD's hosts said unto Joshua, Loose thy shoe from off thy foot; for the place whereon thou standest is holy." Are we to know the power of the leader who is there? Well, then let us get our shoes off! Let us never forget the words of Paul: "I am the slave of Jesus Christ." If our shoes are not off before this leader, we will not know his power. But when we take off our shoes, then, circled by the objective written authority of the book, we will experience the continuity of both the power of God and the leadership of the great One. For the Person at the burning bush, the God of Abraham, Isaac and Jacob, the captain of the Lord's host, Jesus Christ—this One is still with us.

Each of the three great changeless factors that stood at such a crucial time as Joshua's, at the change from the Pentateuchal to the post-Pentateuchal period, continues unbroken. There are changes in history, but these three things go on without changing. We in our battles in the twentieth century have the same book, the same power and the same leader.

three
The Continuity
of the
Covenant

Another historic continuity was exhibited especially clearly at the time of Joshua—the continuity of the Abrahamic covenant. God himself reminded Joshua of the promise God had made to the patriarchs: "Be strong and of a good courage: for unto this people shalt thou divide for an inheritance the land, which I sware unto their fathers to give them" (Josh. 1:6). The promise had been made, and now it was going to be fulfilled.

At the golden calf, when God had said, "This people has revolted against me and deserves my judgment in a total way," Moses pleaded the people's cause: "Remember Abraham, Isaac, and Israel, thy servants, to whom thou swarest by thine own self, and saidst unto them, I will multiply your seed as the stars of heaven, and all this land that I have spoken of will I give unto your seed, and they shall inherit it for ever" (Ex. 32:13). Now as the people enter the land, Joshua, too, looks back to a covenant promise God made to Abraham, Isaac and Jacob: The land was to belong to the Israelites.

The Abrahamic Covenant

Let us study in some detail the Abrahamic covenant, which contained the promise of the land. This was its beginning:

> Now the LORD had said unto Abram, Get thee out of thy country, and from thy kindred, and from thy father's house, unto a land that I will shew thee: and I will make of thee a great nation, and I will bless thee, and make thy name great; and thou shalt be a blessing: And I will bless them that bless thee, and curse him that curseth thee: and in thee shall all families of the earth be blessed. (Gen. 12:1-3)

Abraham was in Ur of the Chaldees when God spoke to him. First God ordered him to leave one geographic location and travel to another geographic location, a place that was going to belong to him. Linked to this was a national blessing: A great nation would descend from him. Second, God told him that he would be a blessing beyond his own race to all the world. These were the terms of this special covenant God made with Abraham around the year 2000.

In order to understand this covenant, however, we have to go back further still, all the way to an event we cannot date but which nevertheless occurred in history, in space and in time. God first spoke to man about a covenant of grace as soon as man had revolted against him. This revolt meant that man could no longer come to God on the basis of works. We may speak, therefore, of *the covenant of works* prior to the Fall and *the covenant of grace* after the Fall. That is, God introduced the covenant of grace because man the rebel could no longer come to him on the basis of his own works.

God first stated the covenant of grace when he cursed the serpent: "And I will put enmity between thee and the woman, and between thy seed and her seed; it shall bruise thy head, and thou shalt bruise his heel" (Gen. 3:15). At this point the person who would fulfill this statement—the "seed" who would come—is not specified beyond the fact that he would be a human being.

Soon, though, this covenant was limited in a special way: "And Adam knew his wife again; and she bare a son, and called his name Seth: For God, said she, hath appointed me another seed instead of Abel, whom Cain slew. And to Seth, to him also there was born a son; and he called his name Enos: Then began men to call upon the name of the LORD [or better, to call themselves by the name of the Lord]" (Gen. 4:25-26). A division of the human race occurred. The first son, Cain, killed his brother Abel, and another son, Seth, was born to take Abel's place. The human race is united—it comes from one ancestor—yet it is divided into two human races, one having turned back to God and the other standing in the flow of the rebellion. The promised one would come from the former strand.

Later, God limited the covenant of grace further, narrowing the lineage of the promised one from the whole human race down to the Semitic people. This occurred in the time of Noah (again, an event of history though one we cannot date). Noah prophesied to his three sons, "Blessed be the LORD God of Shem; and Canaan shall be his servant. God shall enlarge Japheth, and he shall dwell in the tents of Shem; and Canaan shall be his servant" (Gen. 9:26-27). Usually it is considered, and probably quite correctly, that Shem is the ancestor of the Semitic people.

Finally, around 2000 B.C. (the first time we can bring the biblical narrative into a clear relationship with recorded secular history), the covenant of grace was brought down to a specific man, Abraham, and to a specific nation, Israel. Abraham came from the high Sumerian culture. He was called into a different land and became the first Jew.

As we have seen, the covenant God made with Abraham had two aspects. The more important was a spiritual promise: All the world would be blessed through Abraham. This related to the promise that somebody was coming who would crush the serpent's head. Christ, of course, eventually came from Abraham to the whole human race.

The second aspect of the Abrahamic covenant was the national blessing. In addition to the spiritual blessing to the whole world, God promised Abraham, "I will make of thee a great nation" (Gen. 12:2). In relation to the national blessing came a corollary blessing—the promise of the land. If I were making an outline, I would put spiritual blessing as point 1, national blessing as point 2 and the land as point 2a.

In all its parts, this covenant was *unconditional.* Later, God added conditional portions. If the Israelites as a nation were obedient, certain good things would happen (see, for example, Deut. 27—28). If they were disobedient, they would be taken into captivity. We see the same interplay, by the way, in God's dealings with David and Solomon. David was given an unconditional portion—from him would come the Messiah. But Solomon had a conditional portion —if Solomon and his descendants continued with God, the Messianic line would come through them. Since they did not fulfill the condition, the Messianic line through Mary did not descend through Solomon. Christ was born of David, but not Solomon. Mary came through another son of David and Bathsheba, Nathan (Lk. 3:31). The Messiah had to be born of David, and of Abraham, because this was God's unconditional promise. So, while God later added conditional portions, the Abrahamic covenant as a whole could be called *an eternal covenant.*

Let us now study the two aspects of this covenant in more detail.

The Spiritual Portion

Shortly after Christ had died, Peter stood in the temple area and preached to the Jews:

> For Moses truly said unto the fathers, A prophet shall the Lord your God raise up unto you of your brethren, like unto me; him shall ye hear in all things whatsoever he shall say unto you.... Yea, and all the prophets

from Samuel and those that follow after, as many as
have spoken, have likewise foretold of these days. Ye
are the children of the prophets, and of the covenant
which God made with our fathers, saying unto Abraham, And in thy seed shall all the kindreds of the earth
be blessed. Unto you first God, having raised up his
Son Jesus, sent him to bless you, in turning away every
one of you from his iniquities. (Acts 3:22, 24-26)
Peter was teaching that Moses had given a Messianic prophecy: The Christ would come as a prophet parallel to Moses.
That is, Peter first turned the people's minds toward Moses.
The Jews, of course, were well instructed in all this so Peter
only had to say a few words and they understood the flow.
Peter then related Moses' prophecy to the Abrahamic
covenant. Peter's sermon has meaning only in relation to
this covenant. Right away on Pentecost, Peter said that the
Gentiles were going to have a part in the spiritual blessing,
though he seems not to have understood its full import until his experience with Cornelius (Acts 10) and his confron-
tation with Paul (Gal. 2:14).

Then he addressed the people as Jews and said to them,
in effect, "You have an opportunity now, individually, to
enter into the spiritual part of the Abrahamic covenant."
This was a clear indication that not every Jew is under the
spiritual portion of the covenant merely because he is part
of the nation. Each individual must make a personal decision with regard to the Messiah.

Paul emphasized to the Romans that non-Jews, too, can
come under the spiritual portion of the Abrahamic covenant: "Therefore it is of faith, that it might be by grace; to
the end the promise might be sure to all the seed; not to
that only which is of the law [that is, to those who are Jews],
but to that also which is of the faith of Abraham; who is
the father of us all" (Rom. 4:16). Paul was encompassing
both the Jewish and Gentile believers of his day under the
Abrahamic covenant. He tied this up by quoting one of

God's statements to Abraham: "As it is written, I have made thee a father of many nations" (Rom. 4:17).

Paul wrote to the Galatians, "Abraham believed God, and it was accounted to him for righteousness. Know ye therefore that they which are of faith, the same are the children of Abraham. And the scripture, foreseeing that God would justify the heathen through faith, preached before the gospel unto Abraham, saying, In thee shall all nations be blessed" (Gal. 3:6-8). This is the New Testament's exegesis of what Genesis means when it says that the whole world is blessed in Abraham: The blessing is one of forgiveness of sins on the basis of the work of Christ. With it comes the corollary that when we accept Christ as our Savior we become spiritual Jews, Abraham's children in faith. If we are Gentiles, we do not become national Jews. But whether we are Jew or Gentile, we have the blessing of being spiritual children of Abraham when we follow Abraham's example, that is, when we stop calling God a liar and believe him. The first step in believing in Christ, the Messiah, as Savior is believing God.

Two other verses in Galatians reinforce this exegesis: "That the blessing of Abraham might come on the Gentiles through Jesus Christ; that we might receive the promise of the Spirit through faith" (Gal. 3:14), and "If ye be Christ's, then are ye Abraham's seed, and heirs according to the promise" (Gal. 3:29). What promise? The spiritual portion of the Abrahamic promise.

One major way Abraham showed his faith was his willingness to sacrifice his son. In this we have a forecast of the death of Christ and an indication of Abraham's knowledge that more was involved here than the immediate situation, to such an extent that after Abraham had taken his long journey to the place where God had ordered him to go, "Abraham called the name of that place Jehovah-jireh," that is, "The Lord will see, or provide" (Gen. 22:14). The phrase definitely indicates the future: "As it is said to this day, In the mount of the LORD it shall be seen" (Gen. 22:14).

It is intriguing that the place, Moriah, to which Abraham was taken over these many weary miles was exactly the site that later was to be Jerusalem (2 Chron. 3:1). We have to be careful about saying how much Abraham himself understood in all the details, but there was no blind "leap of faith." Abraham had had much contact with God before this, and much knowledge from God before this event. Here was a forecast that something was coming, a forecast that the Lord would especially provide in this place. The whole setting is a picture of the great sacrifice, when God the Father sent the Son, and the Son was willing to go.

In addition to the fact that when we believe the promises of God as Abraham did we become Abraham's spiritual children, Paul emphasized the personal act of faith through which Abraham entered into a relationship with God:

For what saith the Scripture? Abraham believed God, and it was counted unto him for righteousness. . . . And he received the sign of circumcision, a seal of the righteousness of the faith which he had yet being uncircumcised: that he might be the father of all them that believe, though they be not circumcised, that righteousness might be imputed unto them also: and the father of circumcision to them who are not of the circumcision only, but who also walk in the steps of that faith of our father Abraham, which he had being yet uncircumcised. . . . Therefore it is of faith, that it might be by grace; to the end the promise might be sure to all the seed; not to that only which is of the law, but to that also which is of the faith of Abraham; who is the father of us all. (Rom. 4:3, 11-12, 16)

That people were not spiritual Jews just because they were natural Jews was true before Christ as well as after. There were two Israels: those who were born into the national line only and those who believed God and his promises. In talking about the Old Testament Jews Paul said it is "not as though the word of God hath taken none effect. For they are not all Israel, which are of Israel: neither, because they are the seed of Abraham, are they all children" (Rom. 9:6-7). A person did not automatically fall under the spiritual promises to Abraham because he was a member of national Israel.

This will also be true in the future. Speaking of the Jews' destiny as a nation, Paul wrote, "For if the casting away of them be the reconciling of the world, what shall the receiving of them be, but life from the dead?" (Rom. 11:15). I will not exegete this entire verse, but I do want to point out that a time is coming when the nation will be a spiritual, believing Israel. Romans 11:25 adds, "Blindness in part is happened to Israel, until the fulness of the Gentiles be come in." The phrase "in part" is a happy one, for multitudes of individual Jews from the book of Acts onward have believed to become spiritual Jews, as well as natural Jews by birth. Looking to the future of the Jews as a nation, Romans 11:26 says, "And so all Israel shall be saved." And it is in this setting that Romans 11:29 says, "For the gifts and the calling of God are not repented of." As there is a continuity of the book, the power and the divine leader, so there is a continuity of spiritual blessings—in the past, present and future—under the spiritual portion of the Abrahamic covenant.

The National Portion

The national portion of the Abrahamic covenant had a strong relationship to the land. In his first promises to Abraham God used the phrases *unto a land that I will shew thee* and *unto thy seed will I give this land.* And this promise is referred to constantly throughout the Scriptures. David composed a song about it in approximately the year 1000: "Be ye mindful always of his covenant; the word which he commanded to a thousand generations; even of the covenant which he made with Abraham, and of his oath unto Isaac; and hath confirmed the same to Jacob for a law, and to Israel for an everlasting covenant, saying, Unto thee will I give the land of Canaan, the lot of your inheritance" (1 Chron. 16:15-18). David used the term *everlasting covenant* in relation to the Jews as a nation and then quoted immediately the promise about the land. *The lot of your inheritance* could be translated *the cord of your inheritance.* The picture is that the people of Israel have various blessings, like individual beads, but the string which ties the separate beads together is the land of Canaan.

Psalm 105 contains an exact parallel: "He hath remembered his covenant for ever, the word which he commanded to a thousand generations. Which covenant he made with Abraham, and his oath unto Isaac; and confirmed the same unto Jacob for a law, and to Israel for an everlasting covenant: saying, Unto thee will I give the land of Canaan, the lot of your inheritance" (Ps. 105: 8-11). Again, the terms *everlasting covenant* and *the lot [the cord] of your inheritance* are used. Again, the land ties the promises together.

After Abraham had gone into Egypt and returned to Shechem God repeated his promise to Abraham: "For all the land which thou seest, to thee will I give it, and to thy seed for ever. And I will make thy seed as the dust of the earth: so that if a man can number the dust of the earth, then shall thy seed also be numbered. Arise, walk through the land in the length of it and in the breadth of it; for I will give it unto thee" (Gen. 13:15-17). God began by mentioning the land, for this was the heart of his promise. To whom was he going to give it? To the nation forever. I think his seed being "as the dust of the earth" refers to both the national and spiritual seed so Christians, too, fall in this number.

Later, God repeated the promise, this time in a startling way:

And he brought him forth abroad, and said, Look now toward heaven, and tell the stars, if thou be able to number them: and he said unto him, So shall thy seed be. And he believed in the LORD; and he counted it to him for righteousness. And he said unto him, I am the LORD that brought thee out of Ur of the Chaldees, to give thee this land to inherit it. And he said, Lord GOD, whereby shall I know that I shall inherit it? And he said unto him, Take me an heifer of three years old, and a she goat of three years old, and a ram of three years old, and a turtledove, and a young pigeon. And he took unto him all these, and divided them in the midst, and laid each piece one against another: but the birds divided he not. And when the fowls came down upon the carcases, Abram drove them away. And when the sun was going down, a deep sleep fell upon Abram; and, lo, an horror of great darkness fell upon him. And he said unto Abram, Know of a surety that thy seed shall be a stranger in a land that is not theirs, and shall serve them; and they shall afflict them four hundred years; and also that nation, whom they shall serve, will I judge: and afterward shall they come out with great substance. And thou shalt go to thy fathers in peace; thou shalt be buried in a good old age. But in the fourth generation they shall come hither again: for the iniquity of the Amorites is not yet full. And it came to pass, that, when the sun went down, and it was dark, behold a smoking furnace, and a burning lamp that passed between those pieces. In the same day the LORD made a covenant with Abram, saying, Unto thy seed have I given this land, from the river of Egypt unto the great river, the river Euphrates. (Gen. 15:5-18)

This incident turned upon God's response to Abraham's question, "Whereby shall I know that I shall inherit it?" In an important moment, God gave a tremendous answer. I would call this *the cutting of the friendship covenant* between God and Abraham.

The cutting of a friendship covenant was well known in almost every land of the ancient East. To cut a friendship covenant, one took a prescribed kind of animal and cut it in half. The two halves were placed a distance apart, and the two parties walked together between them. This action bound generations of families together forever. Because it was so binding, it was rarely done.

Cutting a friendship covenant was practiced in China as recently as the last century. There a cock was used. Either before walking between the pieces or afterwards, the parties would also take a beautiful piece of tapestry with a cock woven into it and tear it in two. Each family would keep a half. Generations later, when somebody brought to a member of a family a half of a tapestry which matched a half he had, he was bound to provide friendship at any cost. This was both beautiful and profound.

God cut an everlasting covenant of friendship with Abraham. They did not walk between the pieces together, because God is God and Abraham was only Abraham. But God represented himself with a burning lamp of fire, which went between the two pieces and thereby eternally established the covenant. Though I have no way to prove it, I am convinced that when the Bible speaks of Abraham being God's friend (see 2 Chron. 20:7; Is. 41:8; Jas. 2:23) it is referring to the cutting of the friendship covenant.

God reminded Abraham of this covenant when Abraham was ninety-nine years old:

> And I will make my covenant between me and thee, and will multiply thee exceedingly. And Abram fell on his face: and God talked with him, saying, As for me, behold, my covenant is with thee, and thou shalt be a father of many nations. Neither shall thy name any more be called Abram, but thy name shall be Abraham; for a father of many nations have I made thee. And I

will make thee exceeding fruitful, and I will make nations out of thee, and kings shall come out of thee. And I will establish my covenant between me and thee and thy seed after thee in their generations for an everlasting covenant, to be a God unto thee, and to thy seed after thee. And I will give unto thee, and to thy seed after thee, the land wherein thou art a stranger, all the land of Canaan, for an everlasting possession; and I will be their God. (Gen. 17:2-8)

First God mentioned the national promise, then the spiritual one. God again called the covenant "an everlasting covenant," and the promise of the land to the Jews as the Jews once more had a part. Paul interpreted one of the statements to mean that others besides the Jews would fall under the spiritual blessing: "As for me, behold, my covenant is with thee, and thou shalt be a father of many nations." (See Rom. 4:17.)

So over many years God made it abundantly clear to Abraham that a great nation would come from him and that he would give this nation the land of Canaan.

The Promises Repeated

After Abraham died, God reassured Abraham's son Isaac that he would fulfill his promises. Not surprisingly, God began with the land: "Sojourn in this land, and I will be with thee, and will bless thee; for unto thee, and unto thy seed, I will give all these countries, and I will perform the oath which I sware unto Abraham thy father" (Gen. 26:3). He then went on to repeat the spiritual portion: "In thy seed shall all the nations of the earth be blessed" (Gen. 26:4). God spoke the promise to Isaac a second time, though this time the land was not mentioned (Gen. 26:23-24).

The covenant was also made twice with Jacob. Having come into conflict with his brother Esau, Jacob fled the land. At a certain place he stopped for the night. He dreamed that he saw a ladder reaching to heaven, and in the dream God spoke to him. As in his dealings with Abraham and Isaac, God began with the promise of the land: "And, behold, the LORD stood above it, and said, I am the LORD God of Abraham thy father, and the God of Isaac: the land whereon thou liest, to thee will I give it, and to thy seed" (Gen. 28:13). And he also spoke of the spiritual promise: "In thy seed shall all families of the earth be blest" (Gen. 28:14).

God repeated the covenant to Jacob when he was coming back to the land after his years abroad. Though Jacob's name was changed, the covenant retained the same elements: the national blessing and the land.

> And God appeared unto Jacob again, when he came out of Padan-aram, and blessed him. And God said unto him, Thy name is Jacob: thy name shall not be called any more Jacob, but Israel shall be thy name: and he called his name Israel. And God said unto him, I am God Almighty: be fruitful and multiply; a nation and a company of nations shall be of thee, and kings shall come out of thy loins; and the land which I gave Abraham and Isaac, to thee I will give it, and to thy seed after thee will I give the land. (Gen. 35:9-12)

Years later in Egypt, as Joseph, one of Jacob's sons, lay dying, the promise about the land was on his mind: "And Joseph said unto his brethren, I die: and God will surely visit you, and bring you out of this land unto the land which he sware to Abraham, to Isaac, and to Jacob. And Joseph took an oath of the children of Israel, saying, God will surely visit you, and ye shall carry up my bones from hence" (Gen. 50:24-25). Because these were the covenant promises of God and because God is not a liar, Joseph said to his people, "Don't worry. The promise will be fulfilled. God will take you back in due time. I don't want my bones left here in Egypt. Take them with you when you go." This, incidentally, they did.

When the Passover, a new order of worship, was established, the promise of the land was again involved: "And it shall come to pass, when ye be come to the land which the LORD will give you, according as he hath promised, that ye shall keep this service" (Ex. 12:25). To whom did God make the promise that is mentioned? To Abraham, Isaac and Jacob. When the people entered the land, however, their order of worship was to be the Passover celebration and all that God commanded Moses on Sinai concerning worship, rather than patriarchal worship.

At Mount Sinai, as we have seen, the race finally became a nation. For the first time the word *nation* could be used to describe an immediate historic reality: "Now therefore, if ye will obey my voice indeed, and keep my covenant, then ye shall be a peculiar treasure unto me above all people: for all the earth is mine: and ye shall be unto me a kingdom of priests, and an holy nation" (Ex. 19:5-6). At Sinai the people were given the law and the nation was to be a holy nation.

As the people left Sinai all but one piece was in place. They were now a nation, they had the law, they had been given the new order of worship, they had the book (Ex. 17:14). The last of the pieces, the promise of the land, was ready to be put in place. In only a year and two months after being slaves in Egypt, the people were ready to complete the full complex of the promise of God! Then the spies were sent out, and they came back with the majority report that led the people into real rebellion. There was no point in losing the thirty-eight years. The people had only to believe the promises which had been given; instead, they rebelled.

At the end of the wilderness wandering, this unnecessary parenthesis in Jewish history, the Lord said to Moses, "This is the land which I sware unto Abraham, unto Isaac, and unto Jacob, saying, I will give it unto thy seed: I have caused thee to see it with thine eyes, but thou shalt not go over thither" (Deut. 34:4). Moses was able to look at the land, but he was not able to go into it.

As Joshua waited to enter Canaan, the promise concerning the nation and the land that had been repeated over and over again for all these years was a tremendous factor emotionally, theologically and practically.

We can now more fully understand all that was involved as God spoke to Joshua, particularly as we pay attention to the matter of the land.

> Now after the death of Moses the servant of the LORD it came to pass, that the LORD spake unto Joshua the son of Nun, Moses' minister, saying, Moses my servant is dead; now therefore arise, go over this Jordan, thou, and all this people, unto the land which I do give to them, even to the children of Israel. Every place that the sole of your foot shall tread upon, that have I given unto you, as I said unto Moses. From the wilderness and this Lebanon even unto the great river, the river Euphrates, all the land of the Hittites, and unto the great sea toward the going down of the sun, shall be your coast.... Be strong and of a good courage: for unto this people shalt thou divide for an inheritance the land, which I sware unto their fathers to give them. ... Then Joshua commanded the officers of the people saying, Pass through the host, and command the people, saying, Prepare you victuals; for within three days ye shall pass over this Jordan, to go in to possess the land, which the LORD your God giveth you to possess it. (Josh. 1:1-4, 6, 10-11)

Can you imagine the impact Joshua's words had upon the people as they stood looking across the Jordan? Within three days the great promises were going to be fulfilled!

The Gifts of God Are without Repentance

The continuity of the national portion of the covenant did not end with Joshua, or with Jews today, any more than the continuity of the spiritual portion ended with him. We have seen that the spiritual side of the covenant has something to say to the Jews in the Old Testament, to the Jews in the early church, to the Jews of today and the Jews of the future, and to the Gentiles also. The land, too, was tied with the everlastingness of the covenant: "And I will establish my covenant between me and thee and thy seed after thee in their generations for an everlasting covenant, to be a God unto thee, to thy seed after thee. And I will give unto thee, and to thy seed after thee, the land wherein thou art a stranger, all the land of Canaan for an everlasting possession; and I will be their God" (Gen. 17:7-8).

As we have seen, Paul, speaking about the future of the Jews, said that "the gifts and calling of God are without repentance [literally, are not repented of]" (Rom. 11:29). In other words, God is not done with the Jews. He has made promises which he himself has said are everlasting.

Jeremiah, one of the Old Testament prophets, dealt with the everlastingness of the covenant in relation to the land:

Thus saith the LORD, which giveth the sun for a light by day, and the ordinances of the moon and of the stars for a light by night, which divideth the sea when the waves thereof roar; the LORD of hosts is his name: If those ordinances depart from before me, saith the LORD, then the seed of Israel also shall cease from being a nation before me for ever. Thus saith the LORD; If heaven above can be measured, and the foundations of the earth searched out beneath, I will also cast off all the seed of Israel for all that they have done, saith the LORD. (Jer. 31:35-37)

Just as God made an everlasting covenant with nature at the time of Noah—that the order of nature will not be ended throughout this era—he made a covenant with the nation Israel with as great a finality. If one cannot change, the other cannot change.

At a time when, because of the Babylonian and Assyrian captivities, people were saying, "God has cast off the Jews,"

Jeremiah wrote,

Considerest thou not what this people have spoken, saying, The two families which the LORD hath chosen, he hath even cast them off? thus they have despised my people, that they should be no more a nation before them. Thus saith the LORD; If my covenant be not with day and night, and if I have not appointed the ordinances of heaven and earth; then will I cast away the seed of Abraham, Isaac, and Jacob: for I will cause their captivity to return, and have mercy on them. (Jer. 33:24-26)

This prophecy should ram into our thinking that God's promise regarding the nation is indeed without change.

In this Jeremiah passage the captivity mentioned cannot be just the Babylonian captivity because it is related to the covenant with nature, which continues throughout the whole era. Ezekiel, in a prophecy written at approximately the same time, related the covenant to that future day of which Paul spoke, a future in which Israel as Israel will be saved and will come into the same kind of situation as the individual Jews who believed at Pentecost and since: "A new heart also will I give you, and a new spirit will I put within you: and I will take away the stony heart out of your flesh, and I will give you an heart of flesh. And I will put my spirit within you, and cause you to walk in my statutes, and ye shall keep my judgments, and do them" (Ezek. 36:26-27). This relates to the promise of Joel (Joel 2:28—3:1) which was partially fulfilled at Pentecost and which partially remains to be fulfilled.

Clearly, the gifts and calling of God are without repentance in both halves of the Abrahamic covenant—the spiritual and the national.

Was God Unjust?

We are left with one final question—for our century one that is gigantic. Was it unjust for Joshua to drive out the people who were in the land? It is quite clear, as we have seen, that God promised his people this land, but wasn't this unjust to those who were living there already?

During the cutting of the friendship covenant, God said to Abraham, "But in the fourth generation they [Abraham's descendants] shall come hither again" (Gen. 15:16). There was a reason why they had to wait all these years. It was a reason they had nothing to do with: "The iniquity of the Amorites [was] not yet full" (Gen. 15:16). At the same time that God swore he would give the Jews the land, he informed Abraham that the Amorites' iniquity had not yet come to that level of revolt which made it the proper time to deal with it.

Immediately before the time of Joshua, however, Moses said to the people,

> Speak not thou in thine heart, after that the LORD thy God hath cast them out from before thee, saying For my righteousness the LORD hath brought me in to possess this land: but for the wickedness of these nations the LORD doth drive them out from before thee. Not for thy righteousness, or for the uprightness of thine heart, dost thou go to possess their land: but for the wickedness of these nations the LORD thy God doth drive them out from before thee, and that he may perform the word which the LORD sware unto thy fathers, Abraham, Isaac, and Jacob. (Deut. 9:4-5)

Moses was telling the people, "Don't think you are getting the land because you are so good. Rather, it is because the iniquity of the people in the land has come to such a climax. The covenant promise is there but God has waited hundreds of years for the Amorites' cup of iniquity to flow over."

I think of the "cup of iniquity" in a visual way. I imagine myself holding a cup which has water dripping into it. The water does not come quickly, but I keep holding up the cup. Gradually the water rises, and at a certain point it flows over the brim. This is the principle of the judgment of God: Man is in revolt against God, and God waits in longsuffering until every possibility of man's turning back is exhausted. When the iniquity is full, when the cup overflows, God's judgment comes.

This was true at the time of the flood: "And GOD saw that the wickedness of man was great in the earth, and that every imagination of the thoughts of his heart was only evil continually" (Gen. 6:5). Men were in total rebellion against God. Genesis 6:11-12 indicates that "the earth also was corrupt before God, and the earth was filled with violence. And God looked upon the earth, and, behold, it was corrupt; for all flesh had corrupted his way upon the earth." God waited. We do not know how long. Then came the judgment of the flood. When did it take place? When the cup was full.

In the story of Sodom the same principle is reiterated (Gen. 18:20-33). Because Abraham bargained with God on behalf of the city, it almost seems as though Abraham understood this principle with exactitude.

We might paraphrase the biblical account like this. God said to Abraham, "Sodom is utterly wicked! It is time to destroy this rotten city!"

So Abraham responded, "Lord, if there are fifty righteous people there, will you refrain from destroying it?"

"Yes," God replied. "If there are fifty righteous people there, the iniquity is not yet full."

"What if there are forty-five?"

"All right, if there are forty-five, the iniquity is not yet full."

"What about forty?"

"All right."

"Thirty?"

"All right."

"Twenty?"

"All right."

"Ten?"

"Yes, even ten!"

But since not even ten righteous people could be found, Sodom was destroyed. The Sodomites' cup had been filling, filling, filling; and when the iniquity at Sodom reached a certain level, judgment came.

When the Israelites stood on the east bank of the Jordan, the iniquity of the Amorites was full. The sword of Joshua was the sword of God in judgment—an exact parallel to the flood and to the destruction of Sodom.

Many of the Canaanite cities have been dug up, and one can see that the statuettes which were worshipped by the Canaanites at this period were overwhelmingly perverse. The worship was wrapped up not only with complete rebellion against God but with all kinds of sexual sin. The statuettes were as pornographic as some of today's worst pictures! And in its violence their culture became equal to ours. So in Moses' time, God said, "All right, it is time for the judgment." This reminds us that there is "death in the city" in our own culture.

We have here another continuity: the principle that when iniquity and rebellion come to the full, then God judges. Paul related this principle to a time future to the day on which I am writing this: "For I would not, brethren, that ye should be ignorant of this mystery, lest ye should be wise in your own conceits; that blindness in part has happened to Israel, until the fulness of the Gentiles be come in" (Rom. 11:25). If we had this sentence alone, "the fulness of the Gentiles" could mean one of two things: a fullness in either goodness or revolt. In light of the other places where this phrase is used, there can be no doubt about it: Though they have had the blessings of the Christian age, the Gentiles' cup of iniquity will become full. Then the principle will be applied again and the judgment related to the second coming of Christ will fall.

At that time "all Israel shall be saved: as it is written,

There shall come out of Sion the Deliverer, and shall turn away ungodliness from Jacob: for this is my covenant unto them, when I shall take away their sins" (Rom. 11:26-27). God has made a covenant, and all the Jews—all Israel—are going to come to this place of spiritual blessing when the Gentiles' cup of iniquity is full.

Jesus said the same thing: "And they shall fall by the edge of the sword, and shall be led away captive into all nations: and Jerusalem shall be trodden down of the Gentiles, until the times of the Gentiles be fulfilled" (Lk. 21:24). When the iniquity is full, the course of events will be reversed, and a blessing will come to Israel as Israel. When the disciples asked him, "What's it going to be like when you come back and judge?" Jesus replied, "It's going to be like two periods, like the days of Noah and the days of Sodom. When it's like those days, I will come back and judge" (Lk. 17:26-30).

The Scripture insists that, in a time still future to the present ticking of the clock, when the iniquity of the Gentiles is full, a greater Joshua will come and function once more in judgment:

And I saw heaven opened, and behold a white horse; and he that sat upon him was called Faithful and True, and in righteousness he doth judge and make war. His eyes were as a flame of fire, and on his head were many crowns; and he had a name written, that no man knew, but he himself. And he was clothed with a vesture dipped in blood: and his name is called The Word of God. And the armies which were in heaven followed him upon white horses, clothed in fine linen, white and clean. And out of his mouth goeth a sharp sword, that with it he should smite the nations: and he shall rule them with a rod of iron: and he treadeth the winepress of the fierceness and wrath of Almighty God. And he hath on his vesture and on his thigh a name written, KING OF KINGS, AND LORD OF LORDS. (Rev. 19:11-16)

This is the greater Joshua, Jesus Christ. The One who died so that men can escape judgment will be the One who will be the judge. And it is this Christ who stood before Joshua as the captain of the host of the Lord.

A cup filled with iniquity followed by God's judgment—this is the negative side of the covenant of grace. Why did there have to be a covenant of grace? Because man rebelled and could not come to God in his own goodness. Man was under the judgment of God with true moral guilt before God. So God had to give the covenant of grace at the terrible cost of Christ's death because men were justly under God's condemnation and judgment without it.

We have come now to the last of the continuities I wanted to look at before we examine the book of Joshua in detail. Out of the Pentateuch, through the book of Joshua, to the rest of the Bible and to a time future to ourselves, there is a continuity of the patience of God and the judgment which comes when iniquity is full. The books are not balanced in this life. If we live only between birth and death, we must acknowledge that we live not in a moral universe but in an amoral universe. But if a holy God exists, we live in a moral universe, and that is wonderful. But again, this carries with it that insofar as the books are not balanced in this life, there will be the judgment of God in the future.

This brings us back to Joshua at Jericho. There he met the Christ of the cross, the Christ of the Book of Revelation, who is the judge, who told him that Jericho would fall. As we comprehend the continuities of the book, the supernatural power, the supernatural leader and the covenant (including the principle of judgment), we are ready to understand the taking of the land.

four
Rahab

In the last chapter we focused on the continuity of the national portion of the Abrahamic covenant as it flowed down to the time of Joshua and beyond. Is there anything in the crucial moment of history in which Joshua lived which can show us the continuity of the spiritual blessing? Indeed there is: Rahab the harlot.

The Spies' Perspective

While the Israelites were camped at Shittim, Joshua sent two spies across the Jordan. "And they went, and came into an harlot's house, named Rahab, and lodged there" (Josh. 2:1). Why did the two spies go to a harlot's house? The answer is simple: They went where they could easily "get lost," where they could find shelter with some degree of freedom. There is no place like a harlot's house for people coming and going. There is no indication whatever that they went there for any immoral purpose; this simply does not exist in the story.

Rahab gave the spies two things. First, she gave them

shelter. They were filled with thankfulness that she had hid them and saved their lives, not only because they escaped personally but because her help made possible the success of their venture. Second, she spoke the words which provided the key to the spies' report to Joshua:

And she said unto the men, I know that the LORD hath given you the land, and that your terror is fallen upon us, and that all the inhabitants of the land faint [literally, melt] because of you. For we have heard how the LORD dried up the water of the Red sea for you, when ye came out of Egypt; and what ye did unto the two kings of the Amorites, that were on the other side Jordan, Sihon and Og, whom ye utterly destroyed. And as soon as we had heard these things, our hearts did melt, neither did there remain any more courage in any man, because of you: for the LORD your God, he is God in heaven above, and in earth beneath. (Josh. 2:9-11)

In this remarkable set of words Rahab verbalized the truth to these two spies. The spies came to a most unlikely place, and the words of this woman told them exactly what the situation was.

There was a parallel event in the life of Gideon. God told Gideon that Gideon would save Israel from the hand of the Midianites, and Gideon asked for two different signs to confirm this. After responding to Gideon's request, God gave him one more sign that he did not ask for. God told him to go down at night to the camp of the Midianites. So Gideon went down with his servant. Standing on the periphery of the camp, they heard two Midianites talking:

And when Gideon was come, behold, there was a man that told a dream unto his fellow, and said, Behold, I dreamed a dream, and, lo, a cake of barley bread tumbled into the host of Midian, and came unto a tent, and smote it that it fell, and overturned it, that the tent lay along. And his fellow answered and said, This is nothing else save the sword of Gideon the son of Joash, a man of Israel: for into his hand hath God delivered Midian, and all the host. And it was so, when Gideon heard the telling of the dream, and the interpretation thereof, that he worshipped, and returned into the host of Israel, and said, Arise; for the LORD hath delivered into your hand the host of Midian. (Judg. 7:13-15)

As with the two spies and Rahab, what Gideon heard was giving encouragement through the words of an enemy. It convinced him of the final outcome, thus enabling him to say with courage, "There is no question that we are going to be victorious." From the mouth of somebody on "the other side" came a verbalization that completely settled the situation.

The spies had real faith. For when they responded to Rahab's request they told her that her life would be saved *"when* the Lord hath given us the land" (Josh. 2:14). Not *if* but *when*. These men understood that God's promises were going to stand sure. This was a complete contrast to the ten spies at the time of Moses.

Also a great contrast to the failure of thirty-eight years before was the reply the two men gave to Joshua: "Truly the LORD hath delivered into our hands all the land; for even all the inhabitants of the country do faint because of us" (Josh. 2:24). This sounds almost exactly like what Joshua and Caleb had said. The two spies sent to Jericho were faithful, not just in the sense of having good eyes but in the sense of believing the promises of God.

Rahab's Perspective

Rahab was a harlot in a heathen land. Some people have been embarrassed by this and have tried to tone it down, but it is impossible to do so. That is really what she was. It is the only thing the Hebrew word in Joshua 2:1 can mean.

When she had the men in her house, Rahab besought them in this way:

> Now therefore, I pray you, swear unto me by the LORD, since I have shewed you kindness, that ye will also shew kindness unto my father's house, and give me a true token: and that ye will save alive my father, and my mother, and my brethren, and my sisters, and all that they have, and deliver our lives from death. And the men answered her, Our life for your's, if ye utter not this our business. And it shall be, when the LORD hath given us the land, that we will deal kindly and truly with thee. Then she let them down by a cord through the window: for her house was upon the town wall, and she dwelt upon the wall. And she said unto them, Get you to the mountain, lest the pursuers meet you; and hide yourselves there three days, until the pursuers be returned: and afterward may ye go your way. And the men said unto her, We will be blameless of this thine oath which thou hast made us swear. Behold, when we come into the land, thou shalt bind this line of scarlet thread in the window which thou didst let us down by: and thou shalt bring thy father, and thy mother, and thy brethren, and all thy father's household, home unto thee. And it shall be, that whosoever shall go out of the doors of thy house into the street, his blood shall be upon his head, and we will be guiltless: and whosoever shall be with thee in the house, his blood shall be on our head, if any hand be upon him. And if thou utter this our business, then we will be quit of thine oath which thou hast made us to swear. And she said, According unto your words, so be it. And she sent them away, and they departed: and she bound the scarlet line in the window. (Josh. 2:12-21)

There is no mention here of husband or children. Those designated to be saved are of her "father's household." Verse 2:18 shows that none of her family lived with her.

This is consistent with the word Scripture uses to describe her. Later, when Jericho was taken, who did the spies bring out? "Rahab, and her father, and her mother, and her brethren, ... all her kindred. ... Joshua saved Rahab the harlot alive, and her father's household"(Josh. 6:23, 25). We miss the whole point of the story, therefore, if we become embarrassed and soften it: Rahab was a harlot in a heathen land.

But Rahab had two things going for her. First, she had heard something *propositional*. She had heard what had happened in space-time history when the Hebrews came out of Egypt and when they had fought against Sihon and Og, two nearby powers. Second, in her presence were two spies who represented to her the whole Israelite nation. This is one reason why it was important that the two men did not go to her because she was a harlot. To her they were representatives of God's people. And they did not waver in their faith before this woman (Josh. 2:14). What she had was the message and the tangible contact with the two spies.

Surrounding Rahab, however, was a hostile and awesome environment: Jericho, the mighty fortress, with its great walls. Jericho had stood for hundreds of years; it was impregnable, or so its inhabitants thought. So, though Rahab had heard a propositional message and though she had the two spies standing before her, she was still surrounded by a monolithic mentality, an entire world view. She was pressured by a powerful city and an ancient culture continuing on in its normal life—eating, drinking, marrying and so forth. At that moment she could see nothing with her eyes which indicated it would fall.

What did Rahab do? In the midst of this tension, Rahab believed. This is the crux of the story. "I know that the LORD has given you the land," she said. "The LORD your God, he is God in heaven above, and in earth beneath" (Josh. 2:9, 11). Her statement about God was universal and total.

How did she know that? We are not told. Often in Scripture we find that people knew things, though we are not told *how* they came to know them. But Rahab knew! And what she knew was totally against her culture. She believed in a new God, a God totally and diametrically opposed to the gods of Jericho but a God above all other gods, a universal God. In the midst of the Canaanites, the Ammonites, the Amorites—in the midst of their horrible, polluted worship, laden with sex symbols and sex practices—Rahab affirmed a true theological proposition about who God really is.

Abraham in his day believed God and it was counted to him for righteousness. Joshua also made a personal choice: "And if it seem evil unto you to serve the LORD, choose you this day whom ye will serve; whether the gods which your fathers served that were on the other side of the flood [that is, on the other side of the Euphrates] or the gods of the Amorites, in whose land ye dwell: but as for me and my house, we will serve the LORD" (Josh. 24:15). Rahab stood in exactly the same position. Surrounded by those who worshiped the Canaanite and Amorite gods, she made her decision: "By an act of the will, on the basis of the knowledge that I have, I declare in faith that God is the God of heaven above and the earth beneath. He is the universal God."

Peter preached to the Jews on Pentecost that the covenant was fulfilled in the coming of Christ but that each person had to believe individually. As Paul preached throughout the Roman Empire, non-Jews began to believe. At the time of Joshua, Rahab stood in the stream of the spiritual portion of the covenant as a believing non-Jew. She stood where the Gentiles stood in the New Testament when they first believed the gospel in Antioch. She stood exactly where most Christians stand today, for most of us are non-Jewish believers.

This non-Jew believed and passed from the kingdom of the Amorites to the kingdom of the Jews. But she did something much more profound than exchanging one human citizenship for another. She also passed from the kingdom of darkness to the kingdom of God's dear Son. The book of Hebrews makes a tremendous statement about Rahab, paralleling her to other heroes of the faith: "By faith the harlot Rahab perished not with them that believed not, when she had received the spies with peace" (Heb. 11:31). There were those who did not believe, but she did believe; so she did not perish. More than this, she became something that not all the Jews were, because, as we have seen, not all the Jews were spiritual Jews. Many who stood in the natural line of the covenant never partook of the spiritual blessings because they did not make Rahab's choice. So, curiously enough, she who had been a non-Jewish heathen suddenly became not only a part of the nation of Israel but also a part of the true Israel. With one act of faith, she stepped into the nation and beyond many of the Jews themselves to become a member of spiritual Israel.

The Scarlet Cord

In Joshua 2 we also find the interesting story of the scarlet cord. This cord, on which Rahab let the spies escape from her house, was also to be the mark upon her house to show that she was different from all the rest. Though she knew Jericho was not going to fall for a while, she did not waste any time displaying the cord. She did not want time to pass without that mark upon her house. So we can imagine her, as soon as she let the spies down, pulling up the rope and tying it to her window (Josh. 2:21).

In the preaching of the Christian church, all the way back to Clement of Rome (perhaps earlier, but we do not know), this has been taken as a sign of the blood of Christ, the Lamb. One should not be dogmatic about it because the Bible does not explicitly make this connection; nevertheless, many in the church have emphasized over the centuries that the scarlet cord was a mark of something beyond itself.

Because she placed this mark upon her house, she dwelt in safety. This clearly paralleled the Passover lamb. The Israelites killed the Passover lamb, put its blood on their houses and then were perfectly safe as the angel of death passed over Egypt. The mark of the blood covered them and their households. The Passover lamb, of course, was looking forward to the coming Messiah. So there is, after all, a parallel between the cord and the blood of the lamb.

We can imagine Rahab rushing out and gathering all her family into her house upon the city wall. We can imagine her going through the city and calling out, "Hurry! Hurry! Hurry! Come under the mark of the scarlet cord!" Lot did the same thing in Sodom, you remember, but without success. He went throughout the city trying to gather in his family, including his sons-in-law. But they refused and laughed at him, so they died in the city's destruction. In the days of Noah, those who were gathered into the ark were safe. In Jericho, Rahab's family gathered in the house marked by the scarlet cord were safe.

We see the spiritual element of the covenant blessing flowing on. When the children of Israel were about to leave Egypt, they were given the blood of the Passover lamb under which to be safe. When the people were about to enter the land, they were met by a different, but parallel, sign—a red cord hanging from the window of a believer.

Faith in Action

The Bible expressly says that Rahab demonstrated her faith by her works. The spies did not take her away with them. She had to remain in the kingdom of the Amorites between the time when she declared her allegiance to the living God and the time when judgment fell. In Joshua 2 we are reminded forcefully that there was a king in Jericho; and, if he had known what had occurred, undoubtedly he would have killed Rahab in the cruelest fashion he could have thought of: "And the king of Jericho sent unto Rahab, saying, Bring forth the men that are come to thee, which are entered into thine house" (Josh. 2:3). Here was war—war between the king of Jericho and the king of the Jews, that is, between the king of Jericho and God.

In the book of James, Rahab is the only person paralleled to Abraham: "Was not Abraham our father justified by works, when he had offered Isaac his son upon the altar? . . . likewise also was not Rahab the harlot justified by works, when she had received the messengers, and had sent them out another way?" (Jas. 2:21, 25). To properly exegete the book of James, we need to understand that Abraham had faith, but it was a faith open to demonstration. In fact, it was demonstrated at a tremendous cost: He was willing to trust God and to offer his son. Rahab, too, had a faith that had teeth in it, structure to it, strength in it. She was willing to suffer loss to demonstrate that her faith was valid.

This woman Rahab stood alone in faith against the *total* culture which surrounded her—something none of us today in the Western world has ever yet had to do. For a period of time she stood for the unseen against the seen, standing in acute danger until Jericho fell. If the king had ever found out what she had done, he would have become her chief enemy and would have executed her.

Just before the Israelites came out of Egypt, they sacrificed the Passover lamb. They did it "with loins girded, shoes on feet and staff in hand" (Ex. 12:11), and they became pilgrims. One cannot partake of the Passover lamb without being ready to see the world as a place of pilgrimage and war. Rahab is an even greater illustration of our position in regard to this, because until Jericho fell she lived as a "pilgrim" surrounded by her old alien culture.

This is exactly how the Christian lives, and Rahab is a tremendous example for us. Though you and I have stepped from the kingdom of darkness into the kingdom of God's dear Son, we are still surrounded by a culture controlled by God's great enemy, Satan. We must live in it from the moment we accept Christ as our Savior until judgment falls. We, too, are encompassed by one who was once our king but is now our enemy. It is just plain stupid of a Christian not to expect spiritual warfare while he lives in enemy territory.

Rahab: Ancestor of Christ

But there is even more to Rahab's story of the spiritual continuity of the covenant. Joshua 6:25 says of Rahab: "She dwelleth in Israel even unto this day." She lived the rest of her life as a citizen among God's people. Not only that, she married among these people and became an ancestor of Jesus Christ!

Study the genealogy of Jesus as Matthew records it: "And Naasson begat Salmon; and Salmon begat Booz of Rahab; and Booz begat Obed of Ruth; and Obed begat Jesse; and Jesse begat David the king" (Mt. 1:4-6). David, of course, was a forebear of Christ.

Rahab's position is mentioned by implication in the book of Ruth: "Now these are the generations of Pharez: Pharez begat Hezron, and Hezron begat Ram, and Ram begat Amminadab, and Amminadab begat Nahshon, and Nahshon begat Salmon, and Salmon begat Boaz [of Rahab, as Matthew says], and Boaz begat Obed, and Obed begat Jesse, and Jesse begat David" (Ruth 4:18-22). (See also the parallel in 1 Chron. 2, especially vv. 11-12.)

The book of Numbers provides a key to Nahshon's identity. When the tabernacle was raised in the days of Moses (about thirty-nine years before the events involving Rahab), twelve princes came, one from each tribe, and made a special offering. The first one who came was of the tribe of Judah: "And he that offered his offering the first day was Nahshon the son of Amminadab, of the tribe of Judah" (Num. 7:12). So Nahshon was a great prince of the tribe of Judah, and his son, Salmon, married Rahab. Chronologically, it fits; the timing is just right. Isn't that tremendous? The harlot who became a believer became the wife of a prince of Judah!

Unhappily, some people ask, "But is it fitting that this woman should become a princess and an ancestor of Christ?" I would reply with all the strength that is in me: It is most fitting! In having been unfaithful to the Creator, is not the whole human race a harlot? Indeed, it is most fitting that Rahab should stand in the ancestral line of Christ. Matthew mentions five women in the genealogy he records, and moral charges were brought against every one of them. Jesus Christ did not come from a sinless human line. All, including Mary, needed the Savior. Even she said, "My spirit hath rejoiced in God my Saviour" (Lk. 1:47). *All* the men and *all* the women in the ancestral line of Christ needed Christ as their Savior.

After all, Rahab did not stand with the people of God as an unclean harlot. She had come under the blood of the coming Christ and was the harlot cleansed. Is Rahab any worse than we? If it is not fitting that she should be the ancestress of Christ, is it fitting that we should be the bride of Christ? Woe to anybody who has such a mentality as to be upset by Rahab! Such a person does not understand sin, the horribleness of the whole race turning into a prostitute against the living Creator.

We all stand in Rahab's place in the sight of the holy God. Probably we are even worse, for she had little knowledge. There is probably no one reading this book who has as little knowledge as Rahab had when she made her step of faith. We are all sinners. Each one of us is like this woman living up there on the wall. Each of us deserves only one thing—the flaming judgment of God. If it were not for the spiritual portion of the covenant of grace and Christ's death on Calvary's cross, we would all be lost.

If we do not cast ourselves upon Christ and his finished work, then we are not as wise as that harlot in a heathen land. We are under the judgment of God and will stay under it until we do what Rahab did. She believed. She came under the work of the real Passover Lamb, Jesus Christ. And she passed from the midst of unredeemed humanity to redeemed humanity on the basis of his blood.

So it always is. Jesus Christ stands before all men in one of two capacities (there is no third): Either he is Savior or he is Judge. When he stood as captain of the Lord's host, for one woman and her household he was Savior; for the rest of Jericho he was Judge.

Let those of us who have believed in Christ ask God to help us so that our works will prove our faith, even if this means a threat to us, even if this places us in as much danger as it did Rahab. By God's grace, may our faith have such a structure that, even if it is at great cost, even if we are facing danger, we stand fast. Many thousands of our brothers and sisters in Christ are this day facing danger. The great persecutions did not just occur in the past in the land of Caesar. In North Korea, Africa, Vietnam, Laos and other places, Christians are being killed for being Christians. And many more are not always physically killed but "killed" by being alienated from their own families.

It is hazardous to be a Christian in an age like ours, in a culture that is increasingly alienated from God. But if we have believed, even if we are surrounded and threatened by the kingdom of our previous king, the evil one, may our faith be like Rahab's, observable by courage and by works. Rahab blazes abroad as a tremendous example for all of us.

five
Two Kinds
of Memorials

What was happening as Rahab waited in that place of danger with her scarlet cord in the window? What occurred between the time the spies left her and the time Jericho fell?

Soon after the spies had returned to the east side of Jordan and reported to Joshua, Joshua sent officers among the people to prepare them for the great moment of crossing. The ark of the covenant of the Lord was to lead the procession. Because the ark represented the presence of God, there was to be between it and the people a space of 2,000 cubits (about 3,000 feet, or well over half a mile). Finally, Joshua himself told the people, "Sanctify yourselves: for to morrow the LORD will do wonders among you" (Josh. 3:5).

God said to Joshua, "This day I am going to begin to magnify thee in the sight of all Israel, that they may know that, as I was with Moses, so I will be with thee" (Josh. 3:7). After this encouragement God told him how to instruct the priests who would bear the ark. When they came to the brink of the Jordan, they were to stand still in the water.

Then the people would know that God was really with them because, as the priests' feet touched the river, the river would be rolled back. Why? Because "the ark of the covenant of the Lord of all the earth passeth over before you into Jordan" (Josh. 3:11). Joshua promised the people that "as soon as the soles of the feet of the priests that bear the ark of the LORD, the Lord of all the earth, shall rest in the waters of Jordan, that the waters of Jordan shall be cut off from the waters that come down from above; and they shall stand upon an heap" (Josh. 3:13). Though it was the time of flood, the water would stop.

This was, of course, a continuity with what they had experienced when they came out of Egypt, and Joshua, Caleb and those who were children then would have remembered that event well. Now they were going to see a sign which paralleled the parting of the Red Sea. Though God gave the same sign as he had with Moses in order to establish Joshua's authority with the people, there was obviously something much more important at work than either Moses or Joshua. There is a continuity of the power of the Lord. In both cases, the power of the Lord was there.

The First Kind of Memorial: Two Piles of Stones

When all the people had passed over the Jordan, Joshua obeyed some important instructions from God:

The LORD spake unto Joshua, saying, Take you twelve men out of the people, out of every tribe a man, and command ye them, saying, Take you hence out of the midst of Jordan, out of the place where the priests' feet stood firm, twelve stones, and ye shall carry them over with you, and leave them in the lodging place, where ye shall lodge this night. Then Joshua called the twelve men, whom he had prepared of the children of Israel, out of every tribe a man: and Joshua said unto them, Pass over before the ark of the LORD your God into the midst of Jordan, and take you up every man of you a stone upon his shoulder, according unto the number of the tribes of the children of Israel: that this may be a sign among you, that when your children ask their fathers in time to come, saying, What mean ye by these stones? Then ye shall answer them, That the waters of Jordan were cut off before the ark of the covenant of the LORD; when it passed over Jordan, the waters of Jordan were cut off: and these stones shall be for a memorial unto the children of Israel for ever. And the children of Israel did so as Joshua commanded, and took up twelve stones out of the midst of Jordan, as the LORD spake unto Joshua, according to the number of the tribes of the children of Israel, and carried them over with them unto the place where they lodged, and laid them down there. And Joshua set up twelve stones in the midst of Jordan, in the place where the feet of the priests which bare the ark of the covenant stood: and they are there unto this day. For the priests which bare the ark stood in the midst of Jordan, until every thing was finished that the LORD commanded Joshua to speak unto the people, according to all that Moses commanded Joshua: and the people hasted and passed over. And it came to pass, when all the people were clean passed over, that the ark of the LORD passed over, and the priests, in the presence of the people. (Josh. 4:1-11)

These verses describe the first of the two kinds of memorials I want to discuss in this chapter. The Israelites set up *two* piles of twelve stones so that the people could look back to what God had done in the past as a reminder that he had promised to care for them in the future. Christians through the years have often spoken of "stones in the midst of the Jordan." In the beginning of L'Abri Fellowship, we were going through a great number of difficulties, a real spiritual battle. At that time we sent out our first family prayer letter, pointing out where we were being attacked but also mentioning the "stones in the midst of Jordan," God's acts for us in the preceding weeks. It was then—July 30, 1955—that we first held our yearly day of prayer, a practice we have carried out from that day to this.

The first pile of twelve stones, one for each of the tribes, was set up in the bed of the Jordan. Inscribed on a stone in the lake near Geneva is the message, "When you read this, weep." Someone carved this because when the water gets that low the territory is in drought. When you can read the words, then cry, because the country is in trouble. The memorial in Jordan was exactly the opposite. Someone could have written upon it, "When you see this, rejoice and remember." Occasionally, the Jordan gets very low, and the Israelites were able from time to time to see these twelve stones and to recall the great things God had done for them.

The second pile of stones was, in a way, even more exciting. Twelve men each took a stone out of the place where the priests' feet stood firm, put it on his shoulder and carried it out of the river. These stones which bore the marks of the waters of the Jordan stood on the dry land as a perpetual testimony to God's interest in the Jewish people.

During the first night on the west side, the people camped close to the river, at Gilgal. As they looked up at the mountains which rose steeply to the west, their minds must have been filled with questions. But, at the same time, they were in the land, they had taken the twelve stones and the water had rushed back. That night they would have looked at those twelve stones stacked into a pillar (Josh. 4:20) and realized, "God has done something great. We can have tremendous confidence for the future." These stones were a memorial to God's faithfulness, and therefore a reminder of his trustworthiness in the days which lay ahead.

The Jews had been waiting to enter the land since the time of Abraham. These particular people had been wandering in the wilderness for many years, waiting. Now, though the Jordan in flood had stood in their way, they were in the land. They were where Moses himself had not been allowed to go. And they established the first kind of memorial for all generations.

These stone memorials were set up for two purposes. Joshua told the children of Israel at Gilgal,

> When your children shall ask their fathers in time to come, saying, What mean these stones? Then ye shall let your children know, saying, Israel came over this Jordan on dry land. For the LORD your God dried up the waters of Jordan from before you, until ye were passed over, as the LORD your God did to the Red sea, which he dried up from before us, until we were gone over: that all the people of the earth might know the hand of the LORD, that it is mighty: that ye might fear the LORD your God for ever. (Josh. 4:21-24)

First, the stones were to instruct future generations. We can imagine a godly Jew in years to come taking his children to the twelve stones in Gilgal and saying, "Look! These stones were taken up out of the Jordan. I was there. I saw it happen." Then the grandfather would tell the grandchild, and, though the people died off, the story would go on.

Second, the stones were to tell the other nations round-about that this God is different. He really exists; he is a living God, a God of real power who is immanent in the world.

God today gives us, especially at the beginning of our Christian lives or at the start of a Christian work, things that we can remember. This way, when the waves get high, we can look back and see that God has worked, and that helps to give us a faith in the future. It is this work of God in our lives which should be open to observation and should give a testimony to the world round about us that God is mighty and God is different, that God is neither a projection of man's thinking nor a God who cannot move in history. The power of God should also be manifested through the Christian community as a testimony to the world and to the

Christians themselves.

The Ark: The Character and Promises of God

In preceding chapters, we have studied a number of continuities: the written book, the supernatural power, the supernatural leader, the spiritual blessings of the Abrahamic covenant, the national blessings of the Abrahamic covenant and the reverse side of the covenant of grace, judgment. Now we will study two more continuities that were flowing along, both represented by the ark.

"The ark of the covenant of the LORD your God" stood at the center of the narrative we have just discussed. What was the ark? It was a representation of the character of God. The people had no image to worship; in fact, they were commanded not to make an image. One cannot make an image of God, for God is spirit. But God has a character, and the ark was a statement of that character. Basically, the ark was a box with a lid. It contained the law, expressing the fact that God is holy, and on top of it was the propitiatory, the *mercy seat* (to use the beautiful translation that Luther gave us), representing the love of God. God's love covers God's holiness when we come to God in his own way.

The ark was more, however, than a representation of God's character. It was the ark of the *covenant* of the Lord, the ark of the oath and promises of God. Because of his character as shown in the Ten Commandments—he is a holy God and he will not lie—people need not be afraid that he will renege on his promises. Because this is the kind of God he is, he will not turn away; he will not become a liar. As the people watched the ark being carried more than half a mile ahead of them, it represented not only the existence of God and character of God but also the fact that he had made promises which he meant to keep.

In Joshua 3:11 the ark is called "the ark of the covenant of the Lord of all the earth." God is not a localized God but the universal God. His power did not stop when the Israelites crossed the Jordan any more than it ceased when they left Egypt. He is a God who is universal and not localized—in contrast to the heathens' thought of their gods.

In Joshua 4 the words *the ark of the covenant of the Lord* are used over and over again. They are repeated like a chorus. We proceed in the narrative, see another part of the story and then are reminded again that the ark was the external sign of the oath and promises of God. He was showing that he meant to fulfill his promises.

We do not know what happened to the ark. It is conceivable that it was destroyed when Jerusalem was laid waste by Babylon, or it may have been brought back from Babylon and been in the temple when Titus demolished it in 70 A.D. Perhaps the ark did not come to an end. It is not farfetched to think it exists somewhere and will one day reappear. Whatever happened to it, we must understand that what it represented did not end. The covenant and the oath of God (which reaches all the way back to Genesis 3:15) has come up to today through different forms. From the times of Noah and Abraham, sweeping on through the Old Testament into the New, the promises of God will continue right up to the end of this era and beyond it into eternity.

As we see what happened in Joshua's day, we can take heart in the midst of our struggles. The God who kept his oath and promise to the children of Israel at the dramatic moment of their walking over the Jordan and entering the land will keep his word to the very end. As Bunyan's Pilgrim crossed another river, the river Death, the oath and promises of God gave him absolute assurance. Not only in the river Death but in the whole of life, we can count on God to keep his living promises.

The Second Kind of Memorial: Two Living Signs

Not long after the two piles of stones were in place, a second kind of memorial was established at this crucial moment in Jewish history:

And it came to pass, when all the kings of the Amorites, which were on the side of Jordan westward, and all the kings of the Canaanites, which were by the sea, heard that the LORD had dried up the waters of Jordan from before the children of Israel, until we were passed over, that their heart melted, neither was there spirit in them any more, because of the children of Israel. At that time the LORD said unto Joshua, Make thee sharp knives and circumcise again the children of Israel the second time. And Joshua made him sharp knives, and circumcised the children of Israel at the hill of the foreskins. And this is the cause why Joshua did circumcise: All the people that came out of Egypt, that were males, even all the men of war, died in the wilderness by the way, after they came out of Egypt. Now all the people that came out were circumcised: but all the people that were born in the wilderness by the way as they came forth out of Egypt, them they had not circumcised. For the children of Israel walked forty years in the wilderness, till all the people that were men of war, which came out of Egypt, were consumed, because they obeyed not the voice of the LORD: unto whom the LORD sware that he would not shew them the land, which the LORD swear unto their fathers that he would give us, a land that floweth with milk and honey. And their children, whom he raised up in their stead, them Joshua circumcised: for they were uncircumcised, because they had not circumcised them by the way. And it came to pass, when they had done circumcising all the people, that they abode in their places in the camp, till they were whole. And the LORD said unto Joshua, This day have I rolled away the reproach of Egypt from off you. Wherefore the name of the place is called Gilgal unto this day. (Josh. 5:1-9)

Along with the two piles of stones, God gave two living signs, two sacraments. The emphasis in the above quote is on *circumcision*. God commanded Joshua to circumcise the children of Israel, and Joshua carried this out. All those born during the wilderness wanderings, in other words, all those forty years old and younger, had to be circumcised. This was a huge number.

When the circumcision actually occurred, they called the place where they camped that night *Gilgal,* which means in Hebrew "a rolling." A rolling in what way? God said that with the circumcision there was a rolling away of "the reproach of Egypt" which was upon them.

This circumcising was a strange thing for Joshua, a keen military commander, to do. He was incapacitating his whole fighting force, an absolutely unmilitary act. It is silly to march your men right into the teeth of the enemy and then disable them. Joshua did it, nevertheless, because God told him to.

From a human viewpoint Joshua was jeopardizing everything. Why was circumcision so important? In Stephen's speech in the book of Acts we get an answer. Stephen said about Abraham that God "gave him the covenant of circumcision" (Acts 7:8). Circumcision was not just an abstract religious rite but was rooted in what Stephen properly called *the covenant of circumcision,* which originated with Abraham. The reason Joshua's act was so crucial is that before the Israelites began their battles, every man was to have upon his body the mark of the Abrahamic covenant.

We have seen that God repeated the covenant to Abraham a number of times. In one of the last repetitions, God added something new:

Thou shalt keep my covenant therefore, thou, and thy seed after thee in their generations. This is my covenant which ye shall keep, between me and you and thy seed after thee; Every man child among you shall be circumcised. And ye shall circumcise the flesh of your foreskin; and it shall be a token of the covenant betwixt me and you. And he that is eight days old shall be circumcised among you, every man child in your generations, he that is born in the house, or bought with money of any stranger, which is not of thy seed. He that is born in thy house, and he that is bought with thy money, must needs be circumcised: and my covenant shall be in your flesh for an everlasting covenant. And the uncircumcised man child whose flesh of his foreskin is not circumcised, that soul shall be cut off from his people; he hath broken my covenant. (Gen. 17:9-14)

God told Abraham to mark himself and every man child of his household with a covenant token. Previously they had not been marked with an external sign; now they were to take one upon themselves at the command of God. So circumcision had a real meaning. It was the mark of the covenant—God's promises placed on the bodies of the Jewish men.

Notice how fitting this was. The covenant sign to Noah (Gen. 9) was in the sky—the rainbow. Why? Because it was a covenant not only with Noah but with all of nature. It was a covenant with the earth itself. Therefore, the sign was in the proper place. When the covenant of grace flowed on to Abraham, an appropriate sign was again given. To Abraham the covenant was highly personalized, so the sign was placed on his own body and the bodies of his children. God said it was a token of the covenant "between me and you."

Abraham circumcised his household immediately, for Abraham believed God:

And Abraham took Ishmael his son, and all that were born in his house, and all that were bought with his money, every male among the men of Abraham's house; and circumcised the flesh of their foreskin in the selfsame day, as God had said unto him. Abraham was ninety years old and nine, when he was circumcised in the flesh of his foreskin. And Ishmael his son was thirteen years old, when he was circumcised in

the flesh of his foreskin. (Gen. 17:23-25)
Immediately after Isaac was born, he was circumcised as
well (Gen. 21:4).

It was not, then, only those who believed personally or
who would believe that were circumcised. Ishmael, for
example, was circumcised as well as Isaac. The servants,
too, were circumcised. There was an external portion of the
covenant represented in the circumcision. In other words,
the circumcision was related to the national, natural blessings. It marked the Jew as a Jew. This is the first thing we
must understand about circumcision.

Five hundred years later, the Passover was established.
When it was first performed, there was an exact repetition
of what happened at the time of Abraham:

And the LORD said unto Moses and Aaron, This is the
ordinance of the passover: There shall no stranger eat
thereof: But every man's servant that is bought for
money, when thou hast circumcised him, then shall he
eat thereof. A foreigner and an hired servant shall not
eat thereof. In one house shall it be eaten; thou shalt
not carry forth ought of the flesh abroad out of the
house; neither shall ye break a bone thereof. All the
congregation of Israel shall keep it. And when a stranger shall sojourn with thee, and will keep the passover
to the LORD, let all his males be circumcised, and then
let him come near and keep it; and he shall be as one
that is born in the land: for no uncircumcised person
shall eat thereof. (Ex. 12:43-48)

How did a person gain entrance to the Passover? Through
circumcision. The two sacraments were blended here.

The Passover, of course, involved the tremendous promise of the coming redemption of Christ, on which all the
blessings of the covenant rest—both the national and spiritual. They all rest upon Christ's death because they are all
rooted in the covenant of grace. For as man turned from
God in his rebellion, God immediately promised the Mes-

siah; and every good thing that comes to man rests upon God's grace and upon what he promised to do in Jesus Christ. But there is also an external blessing, seen in the fact that Ishmael was circumcised as well as Isaac. It is the same when a person comes into a Christian church and shares in the Christian situation. He may or may not be saved. Granted, he should not be a member of the church if he is not saved; nevertheless, here he is in the midst of the worship service and the ongoing life of the church. He is raised in the family of God or he comes in from the outside, and he shares certain blessings because of his association. Back in the Old Testament there was also an emphasis on the external blessing of the circumcision.

But circumcision was not only connected with the external, national blessing to the Jews as Jews. It also had a strong spiritual overtone. Deuteronomy 10:16 reminds us that circumcision was intended to mean something in the flow of the spiritual side of the Abrahamic covenant: "Circumcise therefore the foreskin of your heart, and be no more stiffnecked." Deuteronomy 30:6 has the same emphasis: "And the LORD thy God will circumcise thine heart, and the heart of thy seed, to love the LORD thy God with all thine heart, and with all thy soul, that thou mayest live."

This teaching was reiterated years later by the prophets. Jeremiah told the people, "Circumcise yourselves to the LORD, and take away the foreskins of your heart" (Jer. 4:4). Speaking to people all of whom were circumcised, Jeremiah was saying, "Don't you understand? There's a spiritual side to circumcision. It is not just your body that is to bear this mark. There is to be a spiritual reality in your life as well."

Jeremiah gave another striking expression of this. He mentioned the various nations that were uncircumcised, those about whom the Jews would proudly say, "You see, we are circumcised; they're not." Then he declared, "All the house of Israel are uncircumcised in the heart" (Jer.

9:26). "Don't forget," Jeremiah warned the people, "circumcision is to be spiritual. It is not only to indicate physically that you are a Jew."

So the circumcision did two things: It marked the Jew as a Jew in the natural flow of history, but it also marked the spiritual side of the covenant, recalling the tremendous fact that Abraham believed God and it was counted to him for righteousness. God gave not only natural promises to Abraham but spiritual promises to the whole world (Gen. 12). Likewise, there were two aspects to uncircumcision. On the national side, if a person was uncircumcised, he was outside the Jewish people. On the spiritual side, he could have the physical circumcision and yet have an uncircumcised heart. As such, he had no part of the spiritual blessing.

Prior to the campaign against Jericho, it was important for Joshua to circumcise the men so they bore the external sign of the covenant. In the book of Exodus we find an exact parallel. Moses was on his way to lead the Israelites out of bondage. He had been away from his people for forty years. He had married a wife who was not a Jew and had male children who were not circumcised. Before he could begin his leadership, something had to happen: "And it came to pass by the way in the inn, that the LORD met him, and sought to kill him. Then Zipporah took a sharp stone, and cut off the foreskin of her son, and cast it at his feet, and said, Surely a bloody husband art thou to me. So he let him go: then she said, A bloody husband thou art, because of the circumcision" (Ex. 4:24-26).

What does this story mean? Simply this: God actually pointed out to Moses that Moses was not ready to lead God's people until the body of his own son was marked with the sign of the covenant of grace. Moses could not bring himself to do it, and so there was a momentary struggle between husband and wife. When Zipporah had performed the rite, Moses could lead the people.

At Gilgal, because the males were uncircumcised, the

Israelites were not ready to fight the battle of the Lord. They must first bear the mark of the covenant. As soon as the people were circumcised, they were ready to proceed.

The Passover

Immediately after the men were circumcised, the second of the sacraments was observed: "And the children of Israel encamped in Gilgal, and kept the passover on the fourteenth day of the month at even in the plain of Jericho" (Josh. 5:10). The two sacraments were brought together again at this moment of history.

And once more we have a strong parallel with Moses. A short time after the mark of circumcision was placed on him, Moses, under God's hand, was the instigator of the Passover. The parallels between Moses and Joshua are amazing and teach us an important lesson. "Years pass," God seems to say, "but throughout history there is a continuity in my dealings with my people. This continuity is rooted in myself—my character, my promises, my covenant."

As with all the other continuities, the continuity of the Passover did not end with Joshua. The Passover is continued in the Lord's Supper. Both signify the same reality:

Now the first day of the feast of unleavened bread the disciples came to Jesus, saying unto him, Where wilt thou that we prepare for thee to eat the passover? And he said, Go into the city to such a man, and say unto him, The Master saith, My time is at hand; I will keep the passover at thy house with my disciples. And the disciples did as Jesus had appointed them; and they made ready the passover. Now when the even was come, he sat down with the twelve. . . . And as they were eating, Jesus took bread, and blessed it, and brake it, and gave it to the disciples, and said, Take eat; this is my body. And he took the cup, and gave thanks, and gave it to them, saying, Drink ye all of it; for this is

my blood of the new testament, which is shed for many
for the remission of sins. But I say unto you, I will not
drink henceforth of this fruit of the vine, until that day
when I drink it new with you in my Father's kingdom.
And when they had sung an hymn, they went out into
the mount of Olives. (Mt. 26:17-20, 26-30)

Jesus was saying, "I'm taking the Passover because, although the time is changing, there is a continuity." Though
there was a change in the external form, there was no
change in the flow of the covenant and no change in the
fact of having an external token. The Passover became the
Lord's Supper. Paul says we are to keep the Lord's Supper
till Jesus returns. The Lord's Supper looks back to Christ's
death and forward to his second coming.

What, then, was the Passover? The Passover also looked
two ways, back to the liberation from Egypt and forward to
the first coming of the Lord as Savior. The Bible clearly
indicates that the Passover was a prophecy of what Jesus
would do. For instance, the Passover lamb had no bone
broken, and John says that no bone of Jesus was broken
while he was on the cross "that the scripture should be fulfilled" (John 19:36). Paul says, "Christ our passover is sacrificed for us" (1 Cor. 5:7).

Remember that in Joshua 5 the sign of circumcision was
given before the Passover was celebrated. We have a similar
continuity today. We have seen in Deuteronomy and Jeremiah that circumcision related to the spiritual portion of
the covenant. Paul picks this up in Romans: "But he is a
Jew, which is one inwardly; and circumcision is that of the
heart" (Rom. 2:29). Of course! All the little bells ring! This
is exactly what Jeremiah said! This is what Deuteronomy
says! Real circumcision is related not just to the natural
blessings in the body, but to the spiritual blessings as well.
True circumcision is of the heart. So just as a circumcised
Israelite could eat the Passover at Gilgal, a person today
who is circumcised in heart is one who can go on to the

Lord's Supper.

Later on in Romans Paul speaks about this even more strongly. Discussing the blessing that came to Abraham on the basis of his faith, he says, "How was it then reckoned? when he was in circumcision, or in uncircumcision? Not in circumcision, but in uncircumcision. And he received the sign of circumcision, a seal of the righteousness of the faith which he had yet being uncircumcised: that he might be the father of all them that believe, though they be not circumcised" (Rom. 4:10-11). Abraham did not have to be circumcised in order to be saved. There may have been as many as twenty-five years between Abraham's first belief in God and his circumcision. In all those years, Abraham was not separated from God. He had believed God, and God had counted it to him for righteousness. "That's just like your justification," Paul is saying.

Yet that does not mean circumcision was unimportant when the right time came. Being uncircumcised, he had been declared righteous; he had become a child of God. But years later a sign and seal was applied to him. In Genesis 17:11, God told Abraham, "You shall circumcise the flesh of your foreskin; and it shall be a token of the covenant betwixt me and you." In other words, "You're already mine, Abraham, but I'm going to give you a token in your flesh." In Romans 4 we find exactly the same thing. What the Hebrew means by *token*, the Greek means by *seal*.

There is a flow between the circumcision of the Old Testament and the baptism of the New. The New Testament speaks of baptism as the Christian's circumcision. In Colossians: "In whom also ye are circumcised with the circumcision made without hands, in putting off the body of the flesh in the circumcision of Christ: having been buried with him in baptism" (Col. 2:11-12). The main flow of the sentence is clear: "In whom also ye are circumcised in the circumcision of Christ, having been buried with him in baptism." We could say it this way (though the previous quote is the literal translation), "You are circumcised by Christian circumcision being baptized."

Abraham was not saved by circumcision; he was already saved. And the New Testament argues, especially in various Pauline sections, that a person does not have to be either circumcised or baptized to be saved. You can be saved without the sign. The book of Romans argues that neither the Jews nor the Gentiles needed the sign of circumcision for their redemption. 1 Corinthians also argues it. Galatians, strongest of all, argues against any legality that would add an external sign such as circumcision or baptism to the way of salvation. Salvation is all by grace, all on the finished work of Jesus Christ. You can add nothing to it—nothing at all.

Nevertheless, Abraham was commanded to take the covenant sign. Moses, too, learned how important the covenant sign was. And God told Joshua, "You have entered the land; now place the covenant sign on the men before they march against Jericho."

So while Rahab was waiting, God was leading his people to establish at Gilgal two kinds of memorials—two piles of stones and two living memorials. When they were in place, Joshua was ready to march toward Jericho.

six

Jericho,
Achan and Ai

This is the story of Jericho. To appreciate its force, we must deliberately put ourselves into the frame of mind that we are looking at space-time history. These events were real happenings; these people were real people, and the book of Joshua portrays the people involved with psychological depth.

Likewise, the geography is real space-time geography. It is especially important for us to picture the geography of the promised land because we are now studying a period of war. Geography has always been important in warfare, even more in those days than in our own. In warfare armies try to take the commanding points, especially the peaks of mountains, because from there they can control the roads, the rivers, the railroads or whatever may be the main way of transporting supplies.

We can think of three campaigns in World War II in which geography affected tactics. When the Germans entered France, their tactic was to drive a wedge into the middle of France and then expand in both directions. When the

Greeks were fighting the Italians, the Italians took the plain and the Greeks took the hills. As a result the Greeks controlled the situation even with less well-armed forces. The English smashed strongholds first and then fanned out into weaker areas. If we combine these three tactics of warfare, we have a picture of the God-given strategy for Joshua's campaign to take the land.

Let us consider, then, some of the geography of the promised land. Standing at the Jordan River, which flows down into the Dead Sea which is far below sea level, one sees in the west steep hills which rise quickly from the valley. Gilgal was somewhere on the river valley, between the river and Jericho. Jericho controlled the way of ascent into the mountains. At the head of the ascent was another fortress, Ai. The descents and ascents were made by old river beds which had carried the torrents down these steep hills. Swiss mountain climbers understand this well because the oldest roads and trails in the Alps follow old river beds. These are steep because the hills are steep. From a military viewpoint, the old river beds in that day were exactly what the railroads were up through the second world war. If the Israelites were going to capture the hill country from which they could control the rest of the land, they would have to press past Jericho, which controlled the lowest part, go up the ascent and take Ai. Then they would be on top of the hill country, able to expand their wedge and control the various parts of the country from there.

God's Strategy against Jericho

First, the Israelites had to defeat Jericho. Through archaeological digs we have a better idea of what Jericho was like than those who read the Bible in years past. Jericho was not a big city; it was only about seven acres in its entirety. What it really was was a fortress—a very strong fortress prepared to resist seige.

Joshua did not take the city merely by a clever, human

military tactic. The strategy was the Lord's:

> Now Jericho was straitly shut up because of the children of Israel: none went out, and none came in. And the LORD said unto Joshua, See, I have given into thine hand Jericho, and the king thereof, and the mighty men of valour. And ye shall compass the city, all ye men of war, and go round about the city once. Thus shalt thou do six days. And seven priests shall bear before the ark seven trumpets of rams' horns: and the seventh day ye shall compass the city seven times, and the priests shall blow with the trumpets. And it shall come to pass, that when they make a long blast with the ram's horn, and when ye hear the sound of the trumpet, all the people shall shout with a great shout; and the wall of the city shall fall down flat, and the people shall ascend up every man straight before him. And Joshua the son of Nun called the priests, and said unto them, Take up the ark of the covenant, and let seven priests bear seven trumpets of rams' horns before the ark of the LORD. And he said unto the people, Pass on, and compass the city, and let him that is armed pass on before the ark of the LORD. (Josh. 6:1-7)

The people were to march for six days around the city, going around it once each day with the priests leading the way. On the seventh day everyone was to march around the city seven times. Then the priests were to blow the rams' horns and the people were to cry out. When this was done, God said, the walls of the city would fall down flat and everyone could ascend up "straight before him."

Since Jericho was a small city, as was normal for the walled cities of that time, the Israelite army was large enough to completely encircle it. So by the time the first troops had marched around the walls, the last troops would just be starting. On the seventh day when the army cried out and the walls fell, all that the soldiers would have to do is march straight ahead to the center of the city and thus capture it from all sides at once.

"You won't even have to scale the walls," God said. "Every fighting man will be able to draw his sword and march straight forward. You will take the whole city with one blow."

Joshua's obedience revealed Joshua's faith:

And it came to pass, when Joshua had spoken unto the people, that the seven priests bearing the seven trumpets of rams' horns passed on before the LORD, and blew with the trumpets: and the ark of the covenant of the LORD followed them. And the armed men went before the priests that blew with the trumpets, and the rereward came after the ark, the priests going on, and blowing with the trumpets. And Joshua had commanded the people, saying, Ye shall not shout, nor make any noise with your voice, neither shall any word proceed out of your mouth, until the day I bid you shout; then shall ye shout. So the ark of the LORD compassed the city, going about it once: and they came into the camp, and lodged in the camp.

And Joshua rose early in the morning, and the priests took up the ark of the LORD. And seven priests bearing seven trumpets of rams' horns before the ark of the LORD went on continually, and blew with the trumpets: and the armed men went before them; but the rereward came after the ark of the LORD, the priests going on, and blowing with the trumpets. And the second day they compassed the city once, and returned into the camp: so they did six days.

And it came to pass on the seventh day, that they rose early about the dawning of the day, and compassed the city after the same manner seven times: only on that day they compassed the city seven times. And it came to pass at the seventh time, when the priests blew with the trumpets, Joshua said unto the

people, Shout; for the LORD hath given you the city.
(Josh. 6:8-16)

Because of the promise of God, because of his experience over the past forty years, Joshua expected the walls to fall. So "Joshua said unto the people, Shout; for the LORD hath given you the city." They had marched for six days in complete silence, but now they were to shout. When the fighting men did shout, the walls fell down and the men marched in.

Was this a direct act of divine intervention? Or did God simply use a principle of vibration, the principle which explains why an opera singer can break a glass by hitting the right note? We do not know, because God has not told us, but it does not matter which is the case. This was God's strategy, and there was a complete miracle in what occurred. God had made a promise, God had given the strategy, and the victory was accomplished.

At this particular moment Joshua remembered Rahab. All this time Rahab had been sitting in her house, surrounded by the power of the Amorite king. Now her deliverance was at hand. On the basis of the promises she had been given, in faith she had felt safe. Now she was to experience her safety in the midst of judgment. "The city shall be accursed," Joshua said (Josh. 6:17). "Accursed" represents only a part of what this word means. The Hebrew word means both "accursed" or "devoted," that is, "given to God." Here it clearly means the latter: "The city shall be devoted, even it, and all that are therein, to the LORD: only Rahab the harlot shall live, she and all that are with her in the house, because she hid the messengers that we sent." In this way, Joshua gave the command for her protection.

Joshua's commands to the people make clear that the city was devoted: "But as for you, only keep yourselves from the devoted thing, lest when you have devoted it ye take of the devoted thing, so would ye make the camp of Israel accursed, and trouble it. But all the silver, and gold, and vessels of bronze and iron, are holy unto Jehovah; they shall come into the treasury of Jehovah" (Josh. 6:18-19, American Revised). The city of Jericho was a sign of the first fruits. In all things the first fruits belonged to God. Jericho was the first fruits of the land; therefore, everything in it was devoted to God.

The tithe, the first fruits, goes back at least to Abraham. It is another continuity which stretches through the Old Testament to us in New Testament times (in the sense that the New Testament commands proportional giving). Just as Abraham brought his tithes, so Jericho was to be the first fruits.

As Jericho was being overrun, Rahab's great moment came: "But Joshua had said unto the two men that had spied out the country, Go into the harlot's house, and bring out thence the woman, and all that she hath, as ye sware unto her. And the young men that were spies went in, and brought out Rahab, and her father, and her mother, and her brethren, and all that she had; and they brought out all her kindred, and left them without the camp of Israel" (Josh. 6:22-23). Here Rahab became completely identified with the people of God. Just as Noah went into the ark and was safe in the midst of the flood, just as Lot was led out of Sodom, just as the Israelites in Egypt marked their houses with the blood of the Passover lamb, so Rahab, on the basis of her belief, was safe in the midst of the judgment of the city of Jericho.

The city was totally burned (Josh. 6:24). It was neither spoiled nor plundered. Nothing was removed. Everything was burned as it stood because Jericho was devoted to God. Utensils and jars stayed in the houses. The grain remained in the grain pits. To give themselves stores during seige, the inhabitants of Jericho had carved huge grain bins out of the center of the rock on which the city stood. Since the Israelites simply burned the city, the fire scorched the top of the grain while the rest remained. As a matter of fact, such grain from very ancient times has been found, has been planted and has grown.

Joshua gave a prophecy about what it would mean to try to build the city again: "Cursed be the man before the LORD, that riseth up and buildeth this city Jericho: he shall lay the foundation thereof in his firstborn, and in his youngest son shall he set up the gates of it" (Josh. 6:26). Later in the Old Testament we find that it was rebuilt, and with just such a tragedy as Joshua prophesied, but we will not deal with that here. (See 1 Kings 16:34.)

Achan's Sin

The people had destroyed Jericho, and the bottom portion of the ascent was completely open. What remained was to take the smaller fortress, Ai, at the top, for then the Israelites would hold the hill country and could begin to expand their wedge. The greater place had fallen with ease; the lesser place stood before them. The seventh chapter of Joshua begins with the word *But,* and stands in antithesis to the sixth, for it tells a tale of defeat.

We can well understand the psychological condition of these people. Everything must have seemed wide open before them. What was coming must have seemed simple. The men who were sent out to look at Ai reported to Joshua: "Let not all the people go up; but let about two or three thousand men go up and smite Ai; and make not all the people to labour thither; for they are but few" (Josh. 7:3). So only three thousand men went up.

The way the story is presented we cannot be certain whether the people were motivated by pride or faith. "God can do it with a small number," they might have said in faith. Or, "It's a small city. We can do it," they could have said in pride. From what follows pride seems to have been the motive, for there was a tremendous defeat. Thirty-six men were killed and the rest were chased down the descent. They had gone up to this steep place above Jericho, and

107

suddenly they were overwhelmed. Those who climb in the mountains can picture the difficulty of making haste down a steep mountain road, falling all over oneself in trying to get down in a hurry.

How could there be defeat? Didn't they have the book? Didn't they have the supernatural power? Didn't they have the supernatural leader? Wasn't it true that the national aspect of the Abrahamic covenant was being fulfilled? Wasn't it true that the spiritual portion of the Abrahamic covenant had functioned in Rahab's life? Didn't the Israelites have the ark of God with which the Jordan River had rolled back? Hadn't they commemorated this marvelous happening with two piles of stones? Hadn't they been circumcised and put themselves under the external sign of the covenant? Hadn't they celebrated the Passover? Hadn't Jericho fallen? How, then, could there be defeat?

We must feel the tremendous upheaval in the mind of these people. If we do, we can understand Joshua's lament:

And Joshua rent his clothes and fell to the earth upon his face before the ark of the LORD until the eventide, he and the elders of Israel, and put dust upon their heads. And Joshua said, Alas, O Lord GOD, wherefore hast thou at all brought this people over Jordan, to deliver us into the hand of the Amorites, to destroy us? Would to God we had been content, and dwelt on the other side Jordan! O Lord, what shall I say, when Israel turneth their backs before their enemies! For the Canaanites and all the inhabitants of the land shall hear of it, and shall environ us round, and cut off our name from the earth: and what wilt thou do unto thy great name? (Josh. 7:6-9)

Joshua tore his clothes. Going up to the ark, which represented the presence of God, he fell on his face and cried aloud: "Here are these people, the Amorites. Their iniquity is full. The cup has overflowed. Only judgment will do. Now they have defeated us, and what is this going to do to your great name, O God?"

God is brusque at times. He is brusque when those who have ample reason to know the answer forget it. So God responded to Joshua in a hard way:

And the LORD said unto Joshua. Get thee up; wherefore liest thou thus upon thy face? Israel hath sinned, and they have also transgressed my covenant which I commanded them: for they have even taken of the accursed thing, and have also stolen, and dissembled also, and they have put it even among their own stuff. Therefore the children of Israel could not stand before their enemies, but turned their backs before their enemies, because they were accursed: neither will I be with you any more, except ye destroy the accursed from among you. (Josh. 7:10-12)

We find God saying to Joshua, "Don't you understand? There is only one reason for this defeat, and you should know what it is. Sin has come among the people of God." How could the defeat be? What caused the difference between the victory at Jericho and the defeat at Ai? Only one thing, and Joshua, remembering what caused the wandering for thirty-eight years in the wilderness, should have recognized its symptom. "Don't you remember that, Joshua? You should not be here on your face. You should be out dealing with sin among the people. For sin has made the difference."

Soon we learn that Achan had taken some of the things that were devoted to God. God told Joshua that the people "have also stolen" (Josh. 7:11). Stolen from whom? From God. Consequently, what Achan did was no small thing. He had not stolen a possession from another man; he had stolen the first fruits.

Therefore, God ordered Joshua, "Up, sanctify the people, and say, Sanctify yourselves" (Josh. 7:13). When the people first entered the land, before they began the conquest, there had come a call to sanctify themselves in the presence of God. Now, in the midst of defeat, there was only one way to return: The people had to sanctify themselves again.

God himself pointed out the man who had sinned. The people came by tribes, and God pointed out the tribe of Judah. Next he pointed out the family, and the household came, man by man, until the one man, Achan, was indicated.

Then followed Achan's instructive explanation of what he had done and what he had stolen: "Indeed I have sinned against the LORD God of Israel, and thus and thus have I done: When I saw among the spoils a goodly Babylonish garment, and two hundred shekels of silver, and a wedge of gold of fifty shekels weight, then I coveted them, and took them; and, behold, they are hid in the earth in the midst of my tent, and the silver under it" (Josh. 7:20-21). Achan thought, "With piles of stuff lying around, who'll know?" So he carted off the booty, dug up the earth under his tent and buried the loot. And he thought nobody knew. But God knew.

While it is wonderful to have an infinite God, this means we must take his omniscience into account in our daily lives. There is nothing we do that God does not know. There is no night so dark, no coal mine so deep, no astronaut so far out in space that God does not know it. God knows every single thought, every single action. He knew when Achan first coveted, and he knew when he carried out his covetousness.

Achan expressly said, "I coveted them." Sin always begins in the mind. As a work of art begins in the mind and then is externalized, so also does sin. It is from the heart, Jesus said, that sin comes. The last commandment of the Ten Commandments is "Do not covet" because coveting comes before every other sin. Before we break any of the other nine, we have coveted internally something either of God's or of another man's. Then we externalize the sin. Achan coveted;

then he stole.

As a result, thirty-six men were killed. Just imagine: Here was a man going up the hill, perhaps in pride but nevertheless in expectancy, and all of a sudden an Amorite took a spear and thrust him through. In the moments before his death he must have been filled with the realization that something had gone wrong. Achan thought he could hide his sin, but these thirty-six men knew when they had been struck down. Soon the whole camp of the Jews knew that the blessing had stopped. At the judgment of Achan everybody knew he had sinned. Jesus said, "The things that are done in darkness will be known in the light" (Lk. 12:3).

What Achan took is also instructive. He took two kinds of things. First, he took two hundred shekels of silver and a wedge of gold of fifty shekels weight. We can understand easily why he took something which had monetary value. But he also took a "goodly Babylonish garment." Why did he bother with this? The Hebrew literally calls it "a mantle of Shinar." Because Shinar is Babylonia the Authorized Version translates it "Babylonian garment." Babylon was one of the great cities of the world. Babylon became the cultural leader of Mesopotamia. It was the mark of success and power. Anything from Babylon was chic. Even in Assyrian times Babylon was a great place. As far as military might was concerned, Babylon was strong in Hammurabi's time and again in Neo-Babylonian times, but it kept its cultural prestige throughout its periods of weakness. In 606 it returned to military greatness and soon overflowed the Jewish nation. At the period of the Israelites' conquest of the promised land, Babylon was weak militarily but still tremendously great in everybody's mind.

So this mantle of Shinar was not just an old shepherd's cloak, but a very stylish garment. It marked somebody as being "in," as really being "a man of the world." This Babylonian garment, therefore, becomes important for understanding the story. Achan bothered to take it because he

111

wanted to be marked with success, to be chic. Achan's sin, then, had two parts: simple theft and prideful desire deep in his heart. What should this teach Christians? Do we struggle against the danger of stealing from God because we want a mantle of Shinar? Does it teach us to beware of affluence, of prestige, of trying to be a VIP?

When judgment came upon Achan, all the people of God joined in the judgment which God directed. All the people had seen the results, so all the people applied the discipline. They stoned Achan and his family (Josh. 7:25). After the nation was cleansed, all the people moved against Ai.

God now sent out the many to defeat Ai for the same reason he sent out Gideon's few—so that men could not boast but had to credit God for the victory. In Gideon's time God emphasized "take just a few" so that the victors could not boast. The people under Joshua had boasted, "We need only a few," and they had lost. So now God said, "You need everybody to take the city." It was the opposite approach, but the same lesson was learned: Man must look to God for the victories, and not boast, or there will be no victories.

The sequence of events at the fall of Ai was completely different from what had happened at Jericho. At Jericho there had been a miracle: The walls had fallen. At Ai there was no miracle. The Israelites had to take the city through the normal processes of war. God is not mechanical but personal. He is not going to deal with every situation in a mechanical way, and we must not reduce him to a series of mechanical acts, as though because God acts one way in one moment he will act the same way in another. We must allow God to be free. God uses many methods. At Jericho there was a miracle; at Ai, none.

We Christians should not be surprised when the Holy Spirit leads us in different ways at different times. He will not contradict his own principles or character as set forth in the Scripture, but he will not act like a machine, always responding to similar situations in exactly the same ways.

When a Christian falls into the idea that because Jericho has been taken one way Ai must be taken the same way, he has stopped thinking of God as personal.

There is another interesting contrast between the destruction of Ai and of Jericho. Jericho, as we saw, was the first fruits to God; therefore, the men were not to touch anything in it. Achan was punished because he had stolen from God. At Ai, this was reversed. The tithe had already been given, so the people were free to take spoil from this city. Tragedy came to Achan and to the people of God because Achan had been impatient. Had he waited obediently, he could have had the blessing.

Ai, like Jericho, was completely overthrown. So now the people controlled both the top and bottom of the gorge. The whole land was open before them.

The Principle of Judgment

As we think of Jericho, Achan and Ai, let us notice a principle. There is a sequence of factors which is relevant to the people of God in all ages. First, Achan stole from God just as a man today might steal by promising to give a tithe and failing to do so. Second, though only one man sinned, the blessing stopped for the people of God corporately. Third, when judgment was applied, victory came. This simple yet profound process explains all the rest of the Old Testament. It explains the period of the judges, the period of kings, the captivities under Assyria and Babylon, the Jews' return from Babylon and the Jews' dispersion in A.D. 70 under Titus. It explains Romans 9—11, which speaks of the Jews turning away from God and yet at a future day coming back to God and once more, as a nation, being the people of God. First comes blessing, then sin enters, then comes judgment. If the people of God return to him after the judgment, the blessing begins again and flows on.

This process is as much a universal as any continuity we

113

have studied so far. It is the principle of God's judgment of his people. It is unchanging throughout Scripture because God really is there. God is a holy God, God loves his people, and God deals with his people consistently. God blesses his people, and one thing can spoil the blessing—sin, either individual or corporate. When either life in the church or doctrine is not cared for, this stops the blessing as much as when an individual sins. Sin among the people of God either diminishes the blessing or brings the blessing to a halt until it is confessed, judged and removed.

Does this continuity really flow into the New Testament, to this side of the cross and Pentecost? Or is this something that applies only in the Old Testament? Achan's sin, we recall, came at the beginning of a new era. The people had received the law of God and a new order of worship; the race had become the nation; the nation was possessing the land. It was important that the people learn at the beginning of this new era that sin is not to be dealt with lightly.

Another new era began at Pentecost. The Holy Spirit was given to all the people of God. In John 7:39 we are told that the Holy Spirit was not given before Pentecost because Christ was not yet glorified. This does not mean that there was no Holy Spirit, that he had not previously worked in regeneration, that he had not come upon prophets, kings and priests in the Old Testament. The Holy Spirit is the third Person of the Trinity. He has always existed and has always been active. But at Pentecost all the believers became priests of God, all the believers were indwelt by the Holy Spirit, and a new era began.

A little later we read:
And when they had prayed, the place was shaken where they were assembled together; and they were all filled with the Holy Ghost, and they spake the word of God with boldness.

And the multitude of them that believed were of one heart and of one soul: neither said any of them

114

that ought of the things which he possessed was his own; but they had all things common. And with great power gave the apostles witness of the resurrection of the Lord Jesus: and great grace was upon them all. Neither was there any among them that lacked: for as many as were possessors of lands or houses sold them, and brought the prices of the things that were sold, and laid them down at the apostles' feet: and distribution was made unto every man according as he had need. And Joses, who by the apostles was surnamed Barnabas, (which is being interpreted, The son of consolation,) a Levite, and of the country of Cyprus, having land, sold it, and brought the money, and laid it at the apostles' feet.

But a certain man named Ananias, with Sapphira his wife, sold a possession, and kept back part of the price, his wife also being privy to it, and brought a certain part, and laid it at the apostles' feet. But Peter said, Ananias, why hath Satan filled thine heart to lie to the Holy Ghost, and to keep back part of the price of the land? Whiles it remained, was it not thine own? and after it was sold, was it not in thine own power? why hast thou conceived this thing in thine heart? thou hast not lied unto men, but unto God. And Ananias hearing these words fell down, and gave up the ghost: and great fear came on all them that heard these things. And the young men arose, wound him up, and carried him out, and buried him.

And it was about the space of three hours after, when his wife, not knowing what was done, came in. And Peter answered unto her, Tell me whether ye sold the land for so much? And she said, Yea, for so much. Then Peter said unto her, How is it that ye have agreed together to tempt the Spirit of the Lord? behold, the feet of them which have buried thy husband are at the door, and shall carry thee out. Then fell she

down straightway at his feet, and yielded up the ghost:
and the young men came in, and found her dead, and,
carrying her forth, buried her by her husband. And
great fear came upon all the church, and upon as many
as heard these things. (Acts 4:31—5:11)

At the beginning of this even greater period of God's redemptive activity exactly the same thing occurred as in the
story of Achan. Achan stole and Joshua reprimanded him,
"You've not stolen from man, Achan. You've stolen from
God." Peter said to the sinning couple, "You have lied to
God." Ananias and Sapphira were not lying to the church;
they were lying to the Holy Spirit. Money was involved, and,
in its own way, a Babylonian garment was too. Achan
wanted to be like the world so he took the Babylonian garment. Ananias and Sapphira wanted a different kind of
garment—social acceptance in the church of God. They
wanted to have the mark of the elite, the mark of the most
spiritual and consecrated. They didn't want to be generous;
they wanted to be thought generous. If the couple had said,
"We sold this possession, and we're giving you such and
such a percentage," everybody in the church would have
said, "That's fine," and God would have said, "Thank you."
But they did not. They put on their own kind of Babylonian garment. This desire can easily become a sin in any
Christian's heart. It is wrong to perform an action merely
to be accepted in our own Christian group. It does not matter how good the act is in itself or how good it looks.

The sin of Ananias and Sapphira was followed by judgment, because sin would have stopped the church's advance. The church had just experienced a second great filling of the Holy Spirit. Power was there—power to face the
lost Graeco-Roman world. If this sin of acting from bad
motivation in order to be superficially accepted by the
church had been allowed to grow in the church's heart, the
whole advance would have been endangered. But after the
judgment, the early church went on in power.

We are not in the beginning of a new era (that beginning was almost two thousand years ago). Can we breathe easily then? Can we count sin lightly, whether individual or corporate, just because this is no longer the opening thrust of the church, as it was after the resurrection of Christ, his ascension and the giving of the Holy Spirit? Can we now have quiet hearts about sin? "No!" the Scripture answers.

We must be careful here. First, not *all* weakness comes because of sin. Our physical or mental weaknesses do not prove that we have sinned. Second, we must avoid falling into a new legalism, either for salvation or for the Christian life. Equally bad, however, is falling into the mentality of antinomianism—the notion that because we are saved by grace on the basis of the finished work of Christ it does not matter how we live. We must resist always equating weakness with sin; we must resist creating a new kind of legalism. But the Word of God makes plain that we equally oppose all forms of antinomianism.

Thus in the book of Joshua we have one more great flowing continuity: the principle of the judgment of the people of God. It runs like this: (1) When we sin, God knows (because he exists and is infinite). (2) When we sin, the blessing slows or stops. It can even stop for a whole group on the basis of the sin of one or a few. (3) There will be judgment either from ourselves in confessing our sin or from God. (4) If we return, the blessing rolls on again.

seven
Mount Ebal and Mount Gerizim

The victorious Israelites now controlled the northern end of the ridge highway that went south by Jerusalem to Hebron. Below them on the east the Jordan River ran parallel to these mountains. Having defeated Ai, the people marched northward on a road which ran over the top of the mountains toward Shechem. They did not have to press through a forest where there was no trail. There was a well-established road. A real culture had been in this land for a long, long time.

Let us imagine ourselves among this great crowd of people marching northwest along the road, the Jordan River on our right. After we have traveled about twenty miles, we see two mountains on our left, Mount Ebal and Mount Gerizim. The former stands north of the latter. One road branches off the main road and runs through the valley between the two mountains, heading toward the city of Samaria, which is approximately seven miles beyond.

Between the two mountains is the city of Shechem. Shechem already had a long history and was important to the Jews. Approximately six hundred years before, Abraham stopped there as he came from Ur and built his first altar to the living God. Jacob, when he was fleeing from Laban, carried to this city the teraphim, his father-in-law's family gods which Jacob's wife had stolen. Joseph sought his brothers here just before going on to Dothan where his brothers sold him into slavery, and Joseph was buried there. Jacob dug a well near Shechem, and at this well Jesus would one day speak to a Samaritan woman (John 4). Later yet, Justin Martyr would be born near here. So space-time history had already begun to weave a web around this place.

Ebal and Gerizim are about a mile and a half apart at the top but only about five hundred yards apart at the bottom. Gerizim reaches to approximately 2,895 feet above sea level, Ebal to 3,077 feet. This means that Gerizim stands about 800 feet above the valley and Ebal about 1,000 feet. The names *Gerizim* and *Ebal* have the same meaning: *barren.*

There are two interesting things about these mountains. First, from the top of Ebal or Gerizim we can see a great deal of the promised land. Second, at one place a natural amphitheater exists and as we stand on the top or on the sides of these mountains, we can see and hear everything that is occurring on both of the mountains and in the valley below. Through the years many people have tested this. They have stood on one of the mountains and had other people stand on other parts of the two mountains or in the valley. As they read something in a loud voice but without amplification, the other persons were able to hear all that was spoken. It is God's own amphitheater.

The Altar on Mount Ebal

Moses, before he died, gave an express command that after the Israelites were in the land they were to go to Ebal and Gerizim. At this place were to occur certain events which were to remind them of their relationship to God. So the people came up the road from the south, turned westward and swarmed over these mountains:

> And all Israel, and their elders, and officers, and their judges, stood on this side of the ark and on that side before the priests the Levites, which bare the ark of the covenant of the LORD, as well as the stranger, as he that was born among them; half of them over against mount Gerizim, and half of them over against mount Ebal; ... with the women, and the little ones, and the strangers that walked with them. (Josh. 8:33, 35)

This was the whole congregation of the people of God, not just the fighting men. None were left at their camp in Gilgal.

God had commanded that Mount Gerizim be marked the mountain of blessing and that the taller mountain, Mount Ebal, be marked as the place of warning, or the place of the curse. God was giving the people a huge object lesson: What happened to them in the land was going to depend, as it were, on whether they were living on Mount Gerizim or Mount Ebal. The people were to hear from Mount Gerizim the blessings which would come to them if they kept God's law and from Mount Ebal the curses which would fall upon them if they did not.

On Ebal and Gerizim the people would be confronted with the law in a very striking fashion, as we shall see, but before the law could be read to them, an altar had to be raised to remind them of an important truth. Speaking in the plain of Moab before his death, Moses had instructed,

> Therefore it shall be when ye be gone over Jordan, that ye shall set up these stones, which I command you this day, in mount Ebal, and thou shalt plaister them with plaister. And there shalt thou build an altar unto the LORD thy God, an altar of stones: thou shalt not lift up any iron tool upon them. Thou shalt build the altar of the LORD thy God of whole stones: and thou shalt offer burnt-offerings thereon unto the LORD

thy God: and thou shalt offer peace-offerings, and shalt eat there, and rejoice before the LORD thy God. (Deut. 27:4-7)

The people followed the command of God:

Then Joshua built an altar unto the LORD God of Israel in mount Ebal, as Moses the servant of the LORD commanded the children of Israel, as it is written in the book of the law of Moses, an altar of whole stones, over which no man hath lift up any iron: and they offered thereon burnt-offerings unto the LORD, and sacrificed peace-offerings. (Josh. 8:30-31)

It is significant that the altar was not built on Gerizim, the mountain of blessing, but on Ebal, the mountain from which was declared what would happen when the people sinned. This was a strong reminder to the people that they were not going to be perfect and that they would therefore need an altar. In this we should hear God saying, "You shouldn't sin. But when you do sin, I will give you a way to return to me, through the altar." So while the people were warned of what would occur when they sinned, they were also taught from the very beginning that there would be a way of return.

We have seen many parallels between the time when Moses began to lead the children of Israel out of Egypt and the beginning of the ministry of Joshua, and here is one more. After the law was given on Sinai, God told the people to build an altar: "An altar of earth thou shalt make unto me, and shalt sacrifice thereon thy burnt-offerings, and thy peace-offerings, thy sheep, and thine oxen: in all places where I record my name I will come unto thee, and I will bless thee. And if thou wilt make me an altar of stone, thou shalt not build it of hewn stone: for if thou lift up thy tool upon it, thou hast polluted it" (Ex. 20:24-25). This special altar was not to have any works of man upon it. In this way it was different from the brass altar that was commanded for the tabernacle. When he gave the Ten Commandments,

God wanted the people to understand and never to forget that an altar does not have value because of what people do to it. In other words, this was a complete negation of all humanism. God was teaching the people, "Build an altar at this crucial moment, and it has to be a special kind. Make it of earth and of stones taken right out of the field. Don't carve beautiful designs on them. Don't even square them. There is to be no human mark upon this altar."

When the Israelites were entering into the land under Joshua, they already had built the brazen altar. Nevertheless, they were returned to the earlier lesson made by the rough altar. On Ebal was to be "an altar of whole stones, over which no man hath lift up any iron" (Josh. 8:31). "Learn the lesson well," God was saying. "I'm bringing you here into the heart of the land. And I am giving you again a special altar so that you will never forget that you cannot come to me on a humanistic level." We are reminded in both Exodus and Joshua that the approach to God must always be through sacrifice and not through the keeping of the law or any other work man may himself do.

According to Paul, the Jews should have understood their lesson. Abraham understood: "For what saith the scripture? Abraham believed God, and it was counted unto him for righteousness. Now to him that worketh is the reward not reckoned of grace, but of debt" (Rom. 4:3-4). Abraham did not try to come to God on the basis of his works because he understood that he was a sinner. He came, rather, on the basis of what God supplied. Paul's argument in Romans 4 is that the Old Testament people of God had to come to God exactly as we do, even though Christ had not yet died. If they tried to come on the basis of humanistic works, they could never make it. God is infinite; man is finite. Man has deliberately sinned; therefore, an infinite chasm of moral guilt exists between God and man. How can man with his good works or his worship cross the gap? He cannot. So Abraham's return to God was not by works, but by the way God prescribed.

Paul speaks even more strongly when he explains why the Jews missed the way. Why did the Old Testament people not come to God? What stood in their way?

But Israel, following after a law of righteousness, did not arrive at that law. Wherefore? Because they sought it not by faith, but as it were by works. They stumbled at the stone of stumbling; even as it is written,

Behold, I lay in Zion a stone of
stumbling and a rock of offence:
And he that believeth on him shall
not be put to shame.

Brethren, my heart's desire and my supplication to God is for them, that they may be saved. For I bear them witness that they have a zeal for God, but not according to knowledge. For being ignorant of God's righteousness, and seeking to establish their own, they did not subject themselves to the righteousness of God. For Christ is the end of the law unto righteousness to every one that believeth. (Rom. 9:31—10:4, ASV)

The reason many of the Old Testament Jews missed their way while Abraham found it is that Abraham came to God on the basis of God's promises of what God himself would do. Because he did not keep the law perfectly, Abraham, as it were, did not try to come to God through Mount Gerizim. He came through Mount Ebal, for he was looking forward to what Christ would do. Paul maintains that the entire series of Old Testament tragedies occurred because the Jews kept trying to come to God through Gerizim, the mountain of blessing, in trying to come through the law, rather than through Mount Ebal. They did not understand that the only way to come to God is not trusting in humanistic works but coming only through sacrifice. Much indeed has been told to the Jews: "Remember, the important thing is the altar!"

When the Assyrians carried away the northern kingdom

into captivity, they transported all kinds of people into the promised land. This mixed group became the Samaritans. The Samaritans hated the Jews. The Samaritans set up their own worship, and, following the thinking of men, made the center of it (amazingly) Mount Gerizim. They were the humanists. When the Samaritans came into the land and were figuring out for themselves how to worship God, they must have thought, "We won't choose Mount Ebal. Who wants to say we're sinners? We'll worship on Mount Gerizim." In other words, they stood in the place of Cain who tried to please God in his own way. And the Samaritans, from that day to this, have worshiped on Mount Gerizim, trying to come to God on the basis of their own works. The only sacrifice going on anywhere in the world today that has any relationship to the Old Testament is carried out each Passover season on Mount Gerizim. The leading Jewish priests from Israel travel to watch the non-Jews, the Samaritans, sacrifice there. They watch with great care because there is some parallel between this and what the Jews did before the temple was destroyed. Undoubtedly, there is a question in many of their minds: "When are we going to begin the sacrifices again?"

Now we can better understand Jesus' conversation at the well with the Samaritan woman. The well stood between Mount Ebal and Mount Gerizim. The woman must have turned and pointed to Mount Gerizim when she said, "Our fathers worshipped in this mountain; and ye say, that in Jerusalem is the place where men ought to worship" (John 4:20). Jesus did not reply, "Yes, you should worship in Jerusalem rather than in Mount Gerizim." He did exactly the opposite. He pointed her away from both Gerizim and Jerusalem, and toward himself. Without going into a big explanation, Jesus implied, "You can't come to God by keeping the law. On the other hand, true worship isn't in Jerusalem either. It's in me. I am the way, the truth and the life. I am the Savior of the world." What Jesus actually did to her, without her realizing all that was involved, was to lift her from Mount Gerizim, where she was trying to come to God on the basis of her own good works (and, like all people, her works were not very good, as you will remember) and to put her on Mount Ebal, where she could come to God in the proper way.

The Law on the Mountains

After the altar was built on Ebal, Joshua "wrote there upon the stones a copy of the law of Moses, which he wrote in the presence of the children of Israel" (Josh. 8:32). The account in Joshua 8 does not tell us by what means the Ten Commandments were copied there, but if we look back into Deuteronomy, we can find out. The words were not carved with a hammer and chisel; they were put on the stones in a much faster way. When Moses gave this command about Ebal and Gerizim,

> Moses with the elders of Israel commanded the people, saying, Keep all the commandments which I command you this day. And it shall be on the day when ye shall pass over Jordan unto the land which the LORD thy God giveth thee, that thou shalt set thee up great stones, and plaister them with plaister: and thou shalt write upon them all the words of this law, when thou art passed over, that thou mayest go unto the land which the LORD thy God giveth thee, a land that floweth with milk and honey; as the LORD God of thy fathers hath promised thee. Therefore it shall be when ye be gone over Jordan, that ye shall set up these stones, which I command you this day, in mount Ebal, and thou shalt plaister them with plaister.... And thou shalt write upon the stones all the words of this law very plainly. (Deut. 27:1-4, 8)

The stones were to be covered with some kind of calcium solution on which the Ten Commandments could be carefully copied. Therefore, the whole process went quickly.

The Israelites just picked up field stones and piled them together. Then somebody covered these big stones with a coating that could be easily etched or painted quickly with a brush as was done on the shards. Someone carefully wrote the Ten Commandments in this coating.

You must see what was involved. You are on Mount Ebal, O humanist man, and here is the law of God. Nobody keeps that, do they? Consequently, what are you going to do? The altar gives you the key. It tells you that the whole approach to God is present in these first and second steps: the remembering of the Ten Commandments and the reality of the altar.

Not only was the altar built and the commandments written but next a section of the writing of Moses was read to all the people, as they crowded onto the sides of the mountain in this natural amphitheater. They could see what was occurring on the tops of the mountains. Now they were going to hear with their ears what would occur if they kept the commandments of God and what would occur if they did not. This was not for salvation because God had already said, "Salvation is to be through the way of the altar." Nevertheless, God had given the people of Israel commandments which were a representation of his character, which is the eternal law of the universe.

Moses had charged the people to have certain tribes stand on Mount Gerizim to bless the people and the remaining tribes stand on Mount Ebal to curse (Deut. 27:11-13). Then the Levites were to read the curses and blessings. Joshua followed the command exactly. After the building of the altar and the copying of the law, "he read all the words of the law, the blessings and cursings, according to all that is written in the book of the law. There was not a word of all that Moses commanded, which Joshua read not before all the congregation of Israel, with the women, and the little ones, and the strangers that were conversant among them" (Josh. 8:34-35).

When Achan sinned, judgment came upon him. We have seen that this is a universal principle: The blessing of God stops when sin enters and flows on again only after the sin is judged. The reading of the blessings and curses forms, therefore, a continuity with the lesson of Achan. Undoubtedly, as the people were on Ebal and Gerizim, that recent event with Achan was very much on their minds. On these mountains it was clearly stated as a general principle that sin must be judged if the blessing is to go on.

Another factor was involved, too: The people needed to be reminded that the blessings of God would be dependent upon their obedience to him. While the Old Testament is full of blessings to the Jews, these blessings were divided into two parts—the unconditional portion and the conditional portion. When God first gave Abraham the Abrahamic covenant, he made it absolutely unconditional: "Now the LORD had said unto Abram, Get thee out of thy country, and from thy kindred, and from thy father's house, unto a land that I will shew thee: and I will make of thee a great nation, and I will bless thee, and make thy name great; and thou shalt be a blessing: and I will bless them that bless thee, and curse him that curseth thee: and in thee shall all families of the earth be blessed" (Gen. 12:1-3). God has taken the Jews; he has made a covenant with them; and he is going to keep it no matter what. As Paul said, looking into the future beyond his day and even beyond our own, "The gifts of God are without repentance."

In the midst of the unconditional promise, however, God put conditional portions. God was not going to turn away from the Jews, but the kind of blessing they would have in the land depended on the extent to which they lived in the light of God's commands. God was pointing this out to the people on Mounts Ebal and Gerizim. He was teaching them, "The whole people must remember this. Many of the blessings, as well as judgment, are conditional. The continuance of the blessings depends upon your keeping my law."

We must remember that God's commands are his propositional statements about his character. They are not arbitrary. God has a character, and his character is the law of the universe. The law is grace in that it reveals what the fulfilling of his character is. God was telling the people that if they lived in the light of his character, then would come the blessing. If they failed to do this, then it would stop.

The Blessings and Curses

We see in the reading of the blessings and curses not only a continuity of the authority of the written, propositional Scriptures but also an emphasis on the fact that bare knowledge is not enough. It was not that the Pentateuch gave these people knowledge, and that was the end of it. This knowledge demanded action. When Joshua took up his leadership, he was told the same thing: "This book of the law shall not depart out of thy mouth; but thou shalt meditate therein day and night, that thou mayest observe *to do* according to all that is written therein: for then thou shalt make thy way prosperous, and then thou shalt have good success" (Josh. 1:8). The normative standard was the law of God; it was not an existential experience (as is often emphasized in the twentieth century), not a non-propositional religious experience (as is said by almost all contemporary liberal theologians). Not at all. What was involved was a propositional, written statement.

The conditional portion of the covenant was being emphasized: It is wonderful for God's people to have the law, but we are then called upon "to do." Our understanding of the rest of the Scriptures turns on our grasp of this point. In the time of the judges, the people did not keep the law of God; so God removed the conditional blessings from them. In the time of the kings, the same thing occurred. The people's disobedience finally caused the captivity of the northern kingdom by the Assyrians and the southern kingdom by the Babylonians. Later, when the people repented, God returned them to the land and the conditional promises again became operative. Later—even with the witness of Jesus—most of the Jews turned completely away, and so in A.D 70 Titus destroyed Jerusalem and the conditional blessing was once more removed. In the future, as we have seen, God will deal with the Jews as a nation again (Rom. 11).

If we understand this, we understand the ebb and flow of history. The Jews remain Jews—they are not wiped out—for God's unconditional promise stands. When men violate the character of God, this is not only sin but stupidity. It is like rubbing your hand over a rough board and getting splinters. For it opposes what we are made to be and what the universe really is. God has revealed his character, and, if God's people keep his character, the conditional blessings stand. Once we understand this, we really understand the flow of history for the Jews.

Moses, speaking before his death, said, "Behold, I set before you this day a blessing and a curse; a blessing, if ye obey the commandments of the LORD your God, which I command you this day: and a curse, if ye will not obey the commandments of the LORD your God, but turn aside out of the way which I command you this day, to go after other gods, which ye have not known" (Deut. 11:26-28). *If!* Both the blessings and the curses are conditional. O man, made in the image of God, O man, who is not merely determined by chemistry, society or psychology, O man, who is a man— you have a choice. Choose!

Hear some of the blessings and curses that were read on the two mountains:

Cursed be the man that maketh any graven or molten image, an abomination unto the LORD, the work of the hands of the craftsman, and putteth it in a secret place. And all the people shall answer and say, Amen.

Cursed be he that setteth light by his father or his

mother. And all the people shall say, Amen.

Cursed be he that removeth his neighbour's landmark. And all the people shall say, Amen.

Cursed be he that maketh the blind to wander out of the way. And all the people shall say, Amen.

Cursed be he that perverteth the judgment of the stranger, fatherless, and widow. And all the people shall say, Amen.

Cursed be he that lieth with his father's wife; because he uncovereth his father's skirt. And all the people shall say, Amen.

Cursed be he that lieth with any manner of beast. And all the people shall say, Amen.

Cursed be he that lieth with his sister, the daughter of his father, or the daughter of his mother. And all the people shall say, Amen.

Cursed be he that lieth with his mother in law. And all the people shall say, Amen.

Cursed be he that smiteth his neighbour secretly. And all the people shall say, Amen.

Cursed be he that taketh reward to slay an innocent person. And all the people shall say, Amen.

Cursed be he that confirmeth not all the words of this law to do them. And all the people shall say, Amen.

And it shall come to pass, if thou shalt hearken diligently unto the voice of the LORD thy God, to observe and to do all his commandments which I command thee this day, that the LORD thy God will set thee on high above all nations of the earth: And all these blessings shall come on thee, and overtake thee, if thou shalt hearken unto the voice of the LORD thy God. Blessed shalt thou be in the city, and blessed shalt thou be in the field. Blessed shall be the fruit of thy body, and the fruit of thy ground, and the fruit of thy cattle, the increase of thy kine, and the flocks of thy sheep. Blessed shall be thy basket and thy store. Blessed shalt thou be when thou comest in, and blessed shalt thou be when thou goest out.

The LORD shall cause thine enemies that rise up against thee to be smitten before thy face: they shall come out against thee one way, and flee before thee seven ways. The LORD shall command the blessing upon thee in thy storehouses, and in all that thou settest thine hand unto; and he shall bless thee in the land which the LORD thy God giveth thee. The LORD shall establish thee an holy people unto himself, as he hath sworn unto thee, if thou shalt keep the commandments of the LORD thy God, and walk in his ways. And all people of the earth shall see that thou art called by the name of the LORD; and they shall be afraid of thee. And the LORD shall make thee plenteous in goods, in the fruit of thy body, and in the fruit of thy cattle, and in the fruit of thy ground, in the land which the LORD sware unto thy fathers to give thee. The LORD shall open unto thee his good treasure, the heaven to give the rain unto thy land in his season, and to bless all the work of thine hand: and thou shalt lend unto many nations, and thou shalt not borrow. And the LORD shall make thee the head, and not the tail; and thou shalt be above only, and thou shalt not be beneath; if that thou hearken unto the commandments of the LORD thy God, which I command thee this day, to observe and to do them: and thou shalt not go aside from any of the words which I command thee this day, to the right hand, or to the left, to go after other gods to serve them. (Deut. 27:15—28:14)

These conditions were, of course, addressed to the Jews as a nation in the land, but they reveal a general principle as well: The people of God must choose whether or not they are going to keep the law. As I have stressed, the whole history of the Jews from this point on turns on their decisions. When they kept the law, the blessings were there. When they turned away, the blessings came to a close until they returned.

Keeping God's Commands

The altar was on the mount of cursing, for salvation cannot come by man's keeping the law. Each one of us must see this. We cannot come to God on the basis of humanistic, religious or moral works. God is an infinite God and we have sinned against him. There was only one way for the Israelites to come, and that was through the altar. The New Testament says this in regard to the work of Christ. Those of us living on this side of Christ must not be foolish like the Samaritans, who tried to come through Gerizim. The only one way to come is through Ebal. We must acknowledge that we have not kept the law.

According to Old and New Testament alike—according to the unconditional spiritual portions of the Abrahamic covenant, the prophecies in the Old Testament which looked forward to Christ, the teaching of Christ himself, and the teaching of Paul and the rest of the apostles—once we have come to God, in the proper way, we stand in unconditional blessing. There is an unconditional portion to me and to you. It reaches all the way back to the beginning of the Bible and is emphasized in the Abrahamic covenant. If we come in the way that God has directed, namely, through the work of Christ, we will never be lost again. We rest in the hands of God. Jesus promises to hold us fast (John 10: 28-29). Because Christ is God his death has infinite value. God's promises are Yea and Amen. Once we have become Christians, we have entered, by faith, by the grace of God, into the spiritual portion of the Abrahamic covenant; and the unconditional promise applies to us—we will never, never, never be lost again.

While this is true, the New Testament also makes plain that for the Christian as for the Old Testament Jew there is also a conditional aspect. The moral law is the expression of

God's character, and we are not to set it aside when we become Christians. Our obedience to it will make a difference in what happens to us both in this present life and in the believers' judgment in the future. So much of Jesus' teaching emphasizes the importance of keeping the law of God! So much of the New Testament emphasizes that we should *think* and then *live* in a conditional as well as an unconditional framework!

How a Christian lives is very important. A Christian should put himself into the arms of his bridegroom, Christ, and let Christ produce his fruit through him. Just as a bride cannot produce natural children until she puts herself into the arms of the bridegroom, so a Christian cannot produce real spiritual fruit except he put himself into the hands of Christ. I can have real spiritual power to the extent that I look to the finished work of Christ and allow him to produce his fruit through me into the external world.

In the Sermon on the Mount Jesus taught much about how a Christian should live. Notice the parallel with the way the Israelites were taught on Mounts Ebal and Gerizim. Jesus was saying to us, the children of God who stand in a spiritual continuity with the Jews, "Yes, I'm going to tell you about an unconditional justification, but there is a conditional portion as well. Think about it because it is important." Important to whom? To the unsaved man? Yes, because it shows him he cannot come by himself; he must come through Christ. To the saved man? Yes, because there is a conditional promise.

I suggest you read this out loud so you can feel it on your own lips and hear it with your own ears:

Take heed that ye do not your alms before men, to be seen of them: otherwise ye have no reward of your Father which is in heaven.

Therefore when thou doest thine alms, do not sound a trumpet before thee, as the hypocrites do in the synagogues and in the streets, that they may have glory of men. Verily I say unto you, They have their reward. But when thou doest alms, let not thy left hand know what thy right hand doeth: that thine alms may be in secret: and thy Father which seeth in secret himself shall reward thee openly.

And when thou prayest, thou shalt not be as the hypocrites are: for they love to pray standing in the synagogues and in the corners of the streets, that they may be seen of men. Verily I say unto you, They have their reward. But thou, when thou prayest, enter into thy closet, and when thou hast shut thy door, pray to thy Father which is in secret; and thy Father which seeth in secret shall reward thee openly.

But when ye pray, use not vain repetitions, as the heathen do: for they think that they shall be heard for their much speaking. Be not ye therefore like unto them: for your Father knoweth what things ye have need of, before ye ask him. After this manner therefore pray ye: Our Father which art in heaven, Hallowed be thy name. Thy kingdom come. Thy will be done in earth, as it is in heaven. Give us this day our daily bread. And forgive us our debts, as we forgive our debtors. And lead us not into temptation, but deliver us from evil: for thine is the kingdom, and the power, and the glory, for ever, Amen. For if ye forgive men their trespasses, your heavenly Father will also forgive you: but if ye forgive not men their trespasses, neither will your Father forgive your trespasses.

Moreover when ye fast, be not, as the hypocrites, of a sad countenance: for they disfigure their faces, that they may appear unto men to fast. Verily I say unto you, They have their reward. But thou, when thou fastest, anoint thine head, and wash thy face; that thou appear not unto men to fast, but unto thy Father which is in secret: and thy Father, which seeth in secret, shall reward thee openly.

> Lay not up for yourselves treasures upon earth, where moth and rust doth corrupt, and where thieves break through and steal: but lay up for yourselves treasures in heaven, where neither moth nor rust doth corrupt, and where thieves do not break through nor steal: for where your treasure is, there will your heart be also. (Mt. 6:1-21)

We do not keep these commands to earn our salvation. Salvation comes only on the basis of the altar, which represented Christ's death in space and time. We must accept salvation with the empty hands of faith. Rather, the commands are the conditional statement in the midst of the unconditional promises. For example, do you as a Christian want to be forgiven existentially by God? Then have a forgiving heart toward other men. That is what Jesus was saying.

Finally, I would remind us of God's command to Joshua about the book:

> This book of the law shall not depart out of thy mouth; but thou shalt meditate therein day and night, that thou mayest *observe to do* according to all that is written therein: for then thou shalt make thy way prosperous, and then thou shalt have good success. (Josh. 1:8)

Notice how this parallels the way Jesus ended the Sermon on the Mount:

> Therefore whosoever heareth these sayings of mine, and *doeth them*, I will liken him unto a wise man, which built his house upon a rock: and the rain descended, and the floods came, and the winds blew, and beat upon that house; and it fell not: for it was founded upon a rock. And every one that heareth these sayings of mine, and doeth them not, shall be likened unto a foolish man, which built his house upon the sand: and the rain descended, and the floods came, and the winds blew, and beat upon that house; and it fell: and great was the fall of it. (Mt. 7:24-27)

On what does successful building depend? It depends first of all upon *hearing* Jesus' words. But if we have heard them and declare them to be the Word of God, what then? Then we must *do* them.

eight
The
Gibeonites

After the reading of the blessings and the curses, the conquest of the land continued. The Israelites were now on top of the mountains; the wedge had been driven in. From this time on the wedge was expanded, first to the south, then to the north.

The Israelites' opponents banded together to oppose this great campaign: "And it came to pass, when all the kings which were on this side Jordan, in the hills, and in the valleys, and in all the coasts of the great sea over against Lebanon, the Hittite, and the Amorite, the Canaanite, the Perizzite, the Hivite, and the Jebusite, heard thereof; that they gathered themselves together, to fight with Joshua, and with Israel, with one accord [literally, with one mouth]" (Josh. 9:1-2). The leaders mounted a united campaign against the people that now stood in such an advantageous position on the mountains. Part of the warfare itself is described in Joshua 10. It can be easily summarized: In a short span of time all the strongholds of the south fell.

The Defeat of the Southern Confederation

The first battle began this way. Jerusalem was the key city in a confederation of five southern city-states. The king of Jerusalem called together the other four kings to attack Gibeon, a city related to the confederation: "Adoni-zedec king of Jerusalem sent unto Hoham king of Hebron, and unto Piram king of Jarmuth, and unto Japhia king of Lachish, and unto Debir king of Eglon, saying, Come up unto me, and help me, that we may smite Gibeon: for it hath made peace with Joshua and with the children of Israel" (Josh. 10:3-4). As the confederation moved against Gibeon, the Gibeonites gave a call for help to the Israelites. (Why Joshua had made peace with Gibeon we will see in a moment.) They sent to Gilgal, the Israelites' permanent base in the valley, to which the women, children and animals had probably returned while the soldiers fought in the highlands, and said, "Slack not thine hand from thy servants; come up to us quickly, and save us, and help us: for all the kings of the Amorites that dwell in the mountains are gathered together against us" (Josh. 10:6). So Joshua departed quickly from Gilgal, and the war was on.

"And the LORD said unto Joshua, Fear them not: for I have delivered them into thine hand; there shall not a man of them stand before thee" (Josh. 10:8). The Israelites had the Word of the Lord with them. They were not functioning on their own without listening to God, as they had in the case of Ai. God said, "This is of me, so go forward without fear and with courage."

They fought a great pitched battle against the confederacy of the five nations, broke the strength of this united army, and put the Amorites to flight. Joshua 10:10 speaks of their fleeing by a way that "goeth up to Beth-horon," while Joshua 10:11 talks about the Amorites' going "down to Beth-horon." At first sight this might seem to be a contradiction, but we know from archaeological studies that there were two Beth-horons, an upper and a lower.

The battle was not won only by the Israelites' valiant fighting. God had said he would be with the people, and, as we pointed out earlier, there should be no stereotypes about how God will act. The fall of Jericho was different from the fall of Ai. The fall of the five kings was again different. God intervened directly through two acts of nature. First, hailstones fell upon the enemy. This added to their confusion in the midst of battle. Second, Joshua spoke to the Lord "in the day when the LORD delivered up the Amorites before the children of Israel, and he said in the sight of Israel,

Sun, stand thou still [literally, be silent] upon Gibeon;
and thou, Moon, in the valley of Ajalon.
And the sun stood still, and the moon stayed,
until the people had avenged themselves upon their
    enemies." (Josh. 10:12-13)

Joshua spoke and God heard him.

"Is not this written in the book of Jasher?" the text then asks. The "book of Jasher" is not part of the inspired Bible, though this portion of it was put into the Bible. The rest of the book is lost. It was apparently not named for a man. As best we can tell, it was a book of poetry that recounted the great acts of God and informed the Jewish people about their heroes. The book of Jasher was mentioned again about four hundred years later, at the time of David. So, though not inspired, it continued to be popular.

When the Israelites came out of Egypt, another poem, "The Song of Moses," was recited. "I will sing unto the LORD, for he hath triumphed gloriously," it began (Ex. 15:1). In Exodus (14:21-29), as in Joshua (10:13), the message is given in prose as well as in poetry. There is no conflict in this. Both texts are talking about a historic event, whether in poetry or prose.

What the text from Joshua is actually saying is that there was a long day. We cannot use the phrase "the sun stood still" to prove that the Jews were ignorant cosmologically.

141

Whether they were or not, the use of this term does not demonstrate that the text is inaccurate, for the simple reason that we today use the same kind of expression. I have never heard a twentieth-century person say when the sun came up in the morning, "The earth has turned far enough to allow me to see the sun." If you said, "The sun is rising" and someone suddenly responded, "How ignorant you are! The earth has turned far enough for you to see the sun," everyone would laugh. The comment would be ridiculous because it is outside the forms in which we normally speak.

I find it strange that some people are upset by the long day. It is not difficult to visualize it. In Switzerland during the summer I can count on light till 9:00 at night. In the middle of winter, however, I must be out of the forest by 6:00, or I am in trouble. In Norway on the longest day of the year the sun does not go down at all! In the North, for days the sun never sets. So we know that the lengths of daylight vary.

How did God do it? We do not know. We might visualize it either of two ways: The earth could have slowed or the earth could have tilted, making the conditions in Israel like those in the north where the sun does not set. There could be other ways that we might not be able to visualize. However it was accomplished, the Bible says that God worked into space-time history to fight for the Israelites.

After the main resistance was broken, the Israelite forces swept on. Throughout the day, one after another of the small city-states fell: Makkedah, Libnah, Lachish, Gezer, Eglon, Hebron and Debir. The whole south fell in one united campaign: The armies were broken, the cities overthrown and the five major kings killed.

So Joshua smote all the country of the hills, and of the south, and of the vale, and of the springs, and all their kings: he left none remaining, but utterly destroyed all that breathed, as the LORD God of Israel commanded. And Joshua smote them from Kadesh-barnea even unto Gaza, and all the country of Goshen, even unto Gibeon. And all these kings and their land did Joshua take at one time, because the LORD God of Israel fought for Israel. And Joshua returned, and all Israel with him, unto the camp to Gilgal. (Josh. 10:40-43)

The wedge was now spread in one direction. The whole southern portion of the land had fallen. This does not mean that all these cities were permanently occupied, but the confederacy was broken and the south was in the hand of the Israelites.

The Deception of the Gibeonites

Having seen the southern campaign successfully completed, let us turn our attention back to Joshua 9. As the Amorite confederacy prepared for its fight against the Israelites, the inhabitants of Gibeon took a drastic step:

And when the inhabitants of Gibeon heard what Joshua had done unto Jericho and to Ai, they did work wilily, and went and made as if they had been ambassadors, and took old sacks upon their asses, and wine bottles, old, and rent, and bound up; and old shoes and clouted upon their feet, and old garments upon them; and all the bread of their provision was dry and mouldy. And they went to Joshua unto the camp at Gilgal, and said unto him, and to the men of Israel, We be come from a far country: now therefore make ye a league with us. And the men of Israel said unto the Hivites, Peradventure ye dwell among us; and how shall we make a league with you? And they said unto Joshua, We are thy servants. And Joshua said unto them, Who are ye? and from whence come ye? And they said unto him, From a very far country thy servants are come because of the name of the LORD thy God: for we have heard the fame of him, and all that he did in Egypt, and all that he did to the two kings of the Amorites, that were beyond Jordan, to Sihon king of Heshbon, and to Og king of Bashan, which was at Ashtaroth. Wherefore our elders and all the inhabitants of our country spake to us saying, Take victuals with you for the journey, and go to meet them, and say unto them, We are your servants: therefore now make ye a league with us. This our bread we took hot for our provision out of our houses on the day we came forth to go unto you; but now, behold, it is dry, and it is mouldy: and these bottles of wine, which we filled, were new; and, behold, they be rent: and these our garments and our shoes are become old by reason of the very long journey. And the men took of their victuals and asked not counsel at the mouth of the LORD. And Joshua made peace with them, and made a league with them to let them live: and the princes of the congregation sware unto them.

And it came to pass at the end of three days after they had made a league with them, that they heard that they were their neighbours, and that they dwelt among them. And the children of Israel journeyed, and came unto their cities on the third day. Now their cities were Gibeon, and Chephirah, and Beeroth, and Kirjath-jearim. And the children of Israel smote them not, because the princes of the congregation had sworn unto them by the LORD God of Israel. And all the congregation murmured against the princes. But all the princes said unto all the congregation, We have sworn unto them by the LORD God of Israel: now therefore we may not touch them. This we will do to them, we will even let them live, lest wrath be upon us, because of the oath which we sware unto them. And the princes said unto them, Let them live; but let them be hewers of wood and drawers of water unto all the congregation; as the princes had promised them.

And Joshua called for them, and he spake unto

them, saying, Wherefore have ye beguiled us, saying, We are very far from you; when ye dwell among us? Now therefore ye are cursed, and there shall none of you be freed from being bondmen, and hewers of wood and drawers of water for the house of my God. And they answered Joshua, and said, Because it was certainly told thy servants, how that the LORD thy God commanded his servant Moses to give you all the land, and to destroy all the inhabitants of the land from before you, therefore we were sore afraid of our lives because of you, and have done this thing. And now, behold, we are in thine hand: as it seemeth good and right unto thee to do unto us, do. And so did he unto them, and delivered them out of the hand of the children of Israel, that they slew them not. And Joshua made them that day hewers of wood and drawers of water for the congregation, and for the altar of the LORD, even unto this day, in the place which he should choose. (Josh. 9:3-27)

The Gibeonites performed an act of deception. The "wine bottles," of course, were skins, and the Gibeonites said, "They are torn. The bread which we took from the oven is now old and dried." They knew very well what had happened to Jericho and Ai, but they never mentioned it. They only mentioned what they would have heard about had they left home a long time ago, that is, they only mentioned what had happened on the east side of the Jordan. And Joshua made a league with them.

The text specifically says that the Israelites did not ask God's counsel. "They received the men by reason of their food" is actually a better translation of the Hebrew; in other words, the Israelites looked at the Gibeonites' food. We can hear the Israelites buzzing among themselves: "Of course, they're telling the truth. Look how old the food is. Look at the bread." We can picture somebody going up and feeling the hard loaves. They did not bother talking to God about the situation, and so they were fooled.

Three days later they found out that they had been taken in, that instead of coming from a far country the Gibeonites lived nearby. So the congregation murmured against the princes: "Why did you do this? You made the oath, and you shouldn't have." Joshua and the other leaders responded that, though it was made in deception, the oath nevertheless held, because it had been made in the name of the Lord. Then Joshua turned to the Gibeonites and said, "There shall none of you be freed from being bondmen, and hewers of wood and drawers of water for the house of my God." "You have asked to be servants, now you will be servants," Joshua told them. They were indeed made servants, but in a special capacity—in the house of God.

The end of this narrative explains the reason for the Gibeonites' action: "It was certainly told thy servants, how that the LORD thy God commanded his servant Moses to give you all the land" (Josh. 9:24). The Gibeonites had understood that God had made a promise to Moses. We can see the force of this when we connect it with the fact that they came "because of the name of the LORD thy God: for we have heard the fame of him" (Josh. 9:9). They had heard about God and what he had done.

Let us quickly put all this together. The Gibeonites sought the Israelites' protection. The Israelites made a league with them without consulting God. Nevertheless, once the oath was made in God's name, it had to be kept. The five-member confederacy said, "Now we're in real trouble. Jericho has fallen; Ai has fallen; and Gibeon, one of the great royal cities, has gone over to the other side." So the confederacy tried to destroy the Gibeonites in order to warn everyone else not to desert to the enemy. The people of Gibeon cried to the Israelites, "You've made a promise to us. This is the moment to fulfill it. Come quickly, or we will be destroyed!" They must have held their breath as they waited to see if the Israelites would honor the oath which had been given because of their own duplicity. But the Israelites did honor the oath (Josh. 10:2-7)

And this was completely right with God. Once the oath was made, God expected the people to keep it. And Joshua did. Many years later, however, the oath was broken. In the days of David there was a three-year famine, and David asked the Lord why. The Lord answered: "It is for Saul, and for his bloody house, because he slew the Gibeonites" (2 Sam. 21:1). When Saul killed the Gibeonites, thereby transgressing the oath made by Joshua about four hundred years before, God responded, "This is serious. Saul broke an oath made in my name, and I hold him accountable."

In the time of Ezekiel, God's people swore in the name of the Lord that they would serve the king of Babylon. Later, because it seemed expedient, they broke their oath. Through the prophet Ezekiel God spoke into the situation:

> As I live, saith the Lord GOD, surely in the place where the king dwelleth that made him king, whose oath he despised, and whose covenant he brake, even with him in the midst of Babylon he shall die. . . . Seeing he despised the oath by breaking the covenant, when, lo, he had given his hand, and hath done all these things, he shall not escape. Therefore thus saith the Lord GOD; As I live, surely mine oath that he hath despised, and my covenant that he hath broken, even it will I recompense upon his own head. And I will spread my net upon him, and he shall be taken in my snare, and I will bring him to Babylon, and will plead with him there for his trespass that he hath trespassed against me. (Ezek. 17:16, 18-20)

The king despised an oath made in God's name. In so doing he did not transgress against the king of Babylon (though that is what the king of Babylon said), but he transgressed against God. God said, "I don't take lightly a king of the Jews making an oath in my name and then breaking it." What was done in the book of Joshua fits into the whole structure of Scripture: An oath made in the name of the God of holiness is to be kept with holy hands.

Psalm 15 states this as a universal principle: "Lord, who shall abide in thy tabernacle? who shall dwell in thy holy hill? ... He that sweareth to his own hurt, and changeth not" (Ps. 15:1, 4). One who swears in the name of God, even if he swears to his own hurt, must keep the oath in order to represent God's character. God is a holy God, and to break an oath made in his name is to transgress, to blaspheme, to caricature the God in whose name the oath is made. Because the Jews were the people of God, they were to have a morality that was not only individual but national. The nation itself was required to keep oaths made in God's name. In light of this principle, we can understand Jesus' warning: "Don't swear lightly because when you swear in the name of God God expects you to be faithful" (Mt. 5:33-37).

Rahab and the Gibeonites

Rahab was a harlot. The Gibeonites were liars. As far as we can tell, they dealt in duplicity without any motion of conscience at all. Bringing their heathen heritage with them, they lied with ease. Why did the Gibeonites come to Joshua? Because they had heard about the Lord and what he had done. And this fact alerts us to the truly important parallels between Rahab and the Gibeonites.

Rahab said this to the spies: "For we have heard how the LORD dried up the water of the Red sea for you, when ye came out of Egypt; and what ye did unto the two kings of the Amorites, that were on the other side Jordan, Sihon and Og, whom ye utterly destroyed. And as soon as we had heard these things, our hearts did melt, neither did there remain any more courage in any man, because of you" (Josh. 2:10-11). The inhabitants of Gibeon, too, were fearful when they heard "what Joshua had done unto Jericho and to Ai ... [and] all that he did to the two kings of the

Amorites, that were beyond Jordan, to Sihon king of Heshbon, and to Og king of Bashan, which was at Ashtaroth" (Josh. 9:3, 10).

In the midst of pagan Jericho Rahab believed on the living God: "And she said unto the men, I know that the LORD hath given you the land" (Josh. 2:9). Strikingly, she affirmed, "For the LORD your God, he is God in heaven above, and in earth beneath" (Josh. 2:11). When she heard what had happened in Egypt and on the other side of Jordan, she said, "This is the living, universal God!" She made a decision on what to her was an adequate testimony. This high and holy expression was something one would never have heard in the heathen world, for there the gods were limited. It does not strike our ears as a surprise because this is the way we think about God, but she was making a declaration of faith which was startling: "I know he isn't a limited god. He's a different kind of a god. He is the LORD your God." She used the Tetragrammaton—God's high and holy name.

Though the Gibeonites' testimony was not as clear as Rahab's, it is apparent that they did believe what they had heard. They said they came "because of the name of the LORD thy God." In Semitic usage a name is a verbalization which represents one's entire character. What the Gibeonites were really saying was, "We came because of who the LORD your God is." Similarly, they spoke of "how that the LORD thy God commanded his servant Moses" (Josh. 9:24). So in the cases of both Rahab and the Gibeonites what they had heard was sufficient to convince them.

Rahab left the kingdom of the enemies of God for the kingdom of the Jews. In making her decision, she pitted herself against her king and her culture. The Gibeonites did likewise. They broke with the confederacy and came over to the people of God. Further, Rahab's act meant that if her old king had found out what she had done he would undoubtedly have killed her. The Gibeonites were actually

149

caught in their defection. The confederacy knew well what they had done. The confederacy, therefore, did in fact come against the Gibeonites to exterminate them.

Rahab the harlot became a part of the people of God: "And Joshua saved Rahab the harlot alive, and her father's household, and all that she had; and she dwelleth in Israel even unto this day" (Josh. 6:25). The whole group of Gibeonites stood in a like circumstance: "And Joshua made them that day hewers of wood and drawers of water for the congregation, and for the altar of the LORD, even unto this day" (Josh. 9:27).

Both Rahab and the Gibeonites proved their loyalty. Rahab helped the spies escape and hung out the scarlet cord. The Gibeonites were faithful to their oath. The Gibeonites were Hivites, a people who remained the enemies of the Israelites, fighting them throughout the period of the judges. And, though the Hivites fought against the Israelites, we find no note that the Gibeonites were unfaithful. So the Gibeonites not only left the confederacy, they broke their normal line. They joined neither their former allies nor their blood relations in the wars that followed. They remained, by an act of choice, in the midst of the people of Israel.

Rahab not only remained a part of the people of God; she married a son of a prince of Judah and became an ancestor of Christ. The Gibeonites, too, had a special place. They remained close to the altar of God. Though they were only hewers of wood and drawers of water, their activity was on behalf of worship of the living God, and it led gradually to a place of religious privilege. When the land was divided, Gibeon was one of the cities given to the line of Aaron. It became a special place where God was known. Approximately four hundred years later, David put the tabernacle in that city. This meant that the altar and the priests were in Gibeon as well. At least one of David's mighty men, those who were closest to him in battle, was a Gibeonite. At that important and solemn moment when Solomon, David's son, ascended the throne, Solomon made burnt offerings at Gibeon. It was there he had his vision, when God spoke to him about his coming rule. Much later still, about five hundred years before Christ, in the time of Zerubbabel, the genealogies of those Jews who returned from captivity under the Babylonians included a list of the Gibeonites. This is especially striking because the names of some who claimed to be Jews were not found in the registry, and they were not allowed to be a part of the Jewish nation. In the days of Nehemiah, the Gibeonites were mentioned as being among the people who rebuilt the walls of Jerusalem. The Gibeonites had come in among the people of God, and hundreds of years later they were still there.

Both Rahab and the Gibeonites stood under the spiritual portion of the covenant of grace. We know from the book of Hebrews that Rahab had salvation. Whether these people who came to Joshua as a group all had individual salvation, we have no way of knowing. But the way God honored these people's faith suggests a tremendous implication: If God, on the basis of the spiritual portion of the covenant of grace, so dealt with Rahab and the Gibeonites when they believed, what would have happened if others had believed? We can also think about the judgment of Nineveh being lifted when its people repented through the preaching of Jonah.

So there really are exact parallels between Rahab the individual and the Gibeonites the corporate unit. Rahab (plus her family) was the only individual saved out of Jericho. The Gibeonites were the only people saved out of the land Rahab believed, left Jericho and came among the people of God. The Gibeonites were the only people in the land who turned to God, and they flowed on through all the years of Jewish history.

Rahab, the Gibeonites and Us
Every Christian, no matter who he is, was once, like Rahab

the prostitute and the Gibeonites the liars, under the wrath and judgment of God. We were all rebels. Not one of us was born good. Not one of us who was raised a Christian automatically became a Christian.

Those who are not Christians remain where Rahab and the Gibeonites stood prior to their identification with the people of God. But Rahab and the Gibeonites believed, and they were accepted. If it is true that God accepted them, how much more true can it be for us who have an open invitation from God. Jesus said, "Whosoever will may come" (see, for instance, John 3:15-16). "Come unto me all ye that labor and are heavy laden," Jesus invited, "and I will give you rest" (Mt. 11:28).

Let us remember that God insisted that the Israelites keep their oath, even though it was made because of the Gibeonites' deception. If God will not tolerate the breaking of an oath made in his name, how much more will he never break his own oath and covenant made to us on the basis of the shed blood and infinite value of Jesus Christ. How secure are we who have cast ourselves upon Christ as our Savior!

For God has made an oath:

For when God made promise to Abraham, because he could swear by no greater, he sware by himself, saying, Surely blessing I will bless thee, and multiplying I will multiply thee. And so, after he had patiently endured, he obtained the promise. For men verily swear by the greater: and an oath for confirmation is to them an end of all strife. Wherein God, willing more abundantly to shew unto the heirs of promise the immutability of his counsel, confirmed it by an oath: that by two immutable things, in which it was impossible for God to lie, we might have a strong consolation, who have fled for refuge to lay hold upon the hope set before us: which hope we have as an anchor of the soul, both sure and stedfast, and which entereth into that within the

vail; whither the forerunner is for us entered, even
Jesus, made an high priest for ever after the order of
Melchisedec. (Heb. 6:13-20)

Here is described the establishment of the Abrahamic
covenant, both its natural and spiritual sides. When men
make an oath, they swear by God. When God made his
promise to Abraham, he swore by himself. There is no one
else by whom God can swear because there is no one greater. He "confirmed it by an oath" the Authorized Version
translates, but the Greek is much stronger, "He interposed
himself by an oath." His oath was himself. It rested upon his
existence and character. Therefore, to the heirs of the
promise he brought two things to bear: the unchangeable-
ness of the act of his will (his counsel), and the fact that he
interposed himself by an oath in his own name. And God
will not lie. Why? Because God is a holy God. Men may draw
back from the idea of judgment, but if God is going to be
worth anything he must be holy. Therefore, the very justice of God should reassure us. He will never break his oath
and word. Never!

Notice the word *we*: "*we* might have strong consolation,
who have fled for refuge to lay hold upon the hope set before us." The book of Hebrews is not just talking about the
Jews. It is talking about believers of all ages, going back to
the time of Abel and flowing on to all who will come under
the promises of God. I love this picture "we who have fled,"
for it carries us back to the Gibeonites and Rahab. Rahab
fled from her place in the kingdom of Jericho to the name
of God. The Gibeonites fled from their race, the Hivites,
and they fled from the confederacy. And we who have
come to Christ have done the same thing: We have fled
from Satan and the world to lay hold of the hope that is set
before us.

Like a boat with an anchor wedged in a rock, we have an
anchor who already stands in the presence of God within
the veil. Who is this anchor? Jesus himself. He is the fore-

runner. We will follow him because we have believed in him. He is within the veil so we will be within the veil.

If the Gibeonites could rely on an oath the Israelites made in the adverse circumstance of the Gibeonites' deception, when the Israelites did not even ask God's counsel, how much more confident can we be in God's oath to us. May we rely upon it. May we cast ourselves upon Christ and be those of a completely quiet heart.

nine
Caleb's Faithfulness

After the Israelites had overthrown the southern strongholds in one mighty effort, they turned to the north. Since the king of Hazor headed the confederacy of the north, he called on the northern kings to do battle, and the Israelites defeated them at the waters of Merom. The north, too, the Israelites took in one campaign, as Joshua 11 describes. In the sense that the strongholds had been broken, the land belonged to them.

The campaigns took 7 years, as we see if we study Joshua 14 carefully. Joshua 14:7 says Caleb was 40 years old when Moses sent him to spy out the land. The wilderness wanderings lasted 38 years. This is a total of 78 years. Joshua 14:10 says that Caleb at the end of the campaigns was 85 years old. Therefore, the campaigns must have taken 7 years. Verse 10 confirms this, for the 38 years of the wandering plus the 7 years of the campaigns equals the 45 years of which Caleb speaks. If the Israelites had entered the land when they could have entered, they would have spent one year coming out of Egypt and 7 years fighting west of Jordan. Thus, in a bit more than 8 years after leaving Egypt they could have had the land. Instead of that, they wasted 38 years.

Chapter 11, like earlier chapters, insists on the continuity of the law of Moses: "As the LORD commanded Moses his servant, so did Moses command Joshua, and so did Joshua; he left nothing undone of all that the LORD commanded Moses. . . . So Joshua took the whole land, according to all that the LORD said unto Moses; and Joshua gave it for an inheritance unto Israel according to their divisions by their tribes. And the land rested from war" (Josh. 11:15, 23). This insistence is important because liberal theologians try to drive a wedge between the Pentateuch and the rest of the Bible. It cannot be done. The rest of the Bible, beginning with Joshua, stands in total continuity with the Pentateuch. Joshua was acting on the basis of God's revelation through Moses.

Joshua 12 is a summary of the total campaign. The summary is divided into two parts: Verses 1-6 describe the campaign under Moses on the east side of the Jordan; verses 7-24, the campaign under Joshua on the west side of the Jordan. When we reach the end of the twelfth chapter, we are halfway through the book, for the book of Joshua is divided into two parts: first, the conquest of the land (chap. 1—12), and then, the settlement of the land and the division to the tribes (chaps. 13—24).

Possessing the Possessions

We turn now to the division of the land among the tribes. The major campaigns were past, but land still remained to be secured: "Now Joshua was old and stricken in years; and the LORD said unto him, Thou art old and stricken in years, and there remaineth yet very much land to be possessed" (Josh. 13:1). There was land to be taken to the north, south, east and west (Josh. 13:2-6). The Israelites had broken the main force of the opposition, but they were still an island in the midst of those who were not the people of God.

Concerning the unconquered people, the Israelites had a promise from God: "Them will I drive out from before the children of Israel: only divide thou it by lot unto the Israelites for an inheritance, as I have commanded thee" (Josh. 13:6). The major campaigns had proven that God indeed is great and that the Israelites, in this supernatural way, could break the heart of the enemy force. Now God promised, "Go on. Divide the land—because I'm going to give you the strength to clear it up and to *possess your possession.*"

Suddenly, however, comes a new note: the failure of the people of God to possess their possessions. Though it lay open before them, they simply did not take hold of that which was theirs to hold. Later Joshua said to the children of Israel, "How long are ye slack to go to possess the land, which the LORD God of your fathers hath given you?" (Josh. 18:3). In other words, "It's yours! Why don't you go and get it?"

There were two reasons for the people's failure. The first was not their fault. For a time they could not. For instance, "As for the Jebusites the inhabitants of Jerusalem, the children of Judah could not drive them out: but the Jebusites dwell with the children of Judah at Jerusalem unto this day" (Josh. 15:63). And, "The children of Manasseh could not drive out the inhabitants of those cities; but the Canaanites would dwell in that land" (Josh. 17:12). But this was not the primary problem, for Joshua 17:13 says, "Yet it came to pass, when the children of Israel were waxen strong, that they put the Canaanites to tribute; but did not utterly drive them out." Though there was a time when they could not vanquish them, when they did become strong enough to drive them out, they did not do so. Rather, they put them under tribute. This was their own fault.

The people of God did not go on to do what God told

them to do for two reasons. First, they wanted peace at any cost and in spite of God's commands; second, they wanted wealth. They were practical materialists. For the sake of ease and money, they did not go forward and do what God told them to do. "Tribute! Tribute! Tribute!" they demanded. And they let the people stay in the land. And through the time of the judges and beyond, instead of gaining ground the Israelites slowly lost it, because they had not possessed their possessions on the basis of God's promise.

Does that sound up to date? These were people who would rather have affluence than possess their possessions under the promises of God. Had God lost his power? Had God reneged on his promise? Was he unable to keep it? Not a bit. God's power was still there. The iron chariots of the enemy should have been no detriment. In Deborah's day the battle was won in the valley plain where the chariots were most useful. All the land was theirs, but, through their lack of faith and their disobedience, they did not make it theirs. The desire for peace and tribute stood in the way. Therefore, on the basis of the conditional portion of the covenant of God, the blessings stopped.

Caleb Remains Faithful

In contrast, happily, somebody did possess his possessions:
Then the children of Judah came unto Joshua in Gilgal: and Caleb the son of Jephunneh the Kenezite said unto him, Thou knowest the thing that the LORD said unto Moses the man of God concerning me and thee in Kadesh-barnea. Forty years old was I when Moses the servant of the LORD sent me from Kadesh-barnea to espy out the land; and I brought him word again as it was in mine heart. Nevertheless my brethren that went up with me made the heart of the people melt: but I wholly followed the LORD my God. And Moses sware on that day, saying, Surely the land whereon thy feet have trodden shall be thine inheritance, and thy chil-

dren's for ever, because thou hast wholly followed the
LORD my God. And now, behold, the LORD hath
kept me alive, as he said, these forty and five years,
even since the LORD spake this word unto Moses,
while the children of Israel wandered in the wilderness: and now, lo, I am this day fourscore and five
years old. As yet I am as strong this day as I was in the
day that Moses sent me: as my strength was then, even
so is my strength now, for war, both to go out, and to
come in. Now therefore give me this mountain, whereof the LORD spake in that day; for thou heardest in
that day how the Anakims were there, and that the
cities were great and fenced: if so be the LORD will be
with me, then I shall be able to drive them out, as the
LORD said.

And Joshua blessed him, and gave unto Caleb the
son of Jephunneh Hebron for an inheritance. Hebron therefore became the inheritance of Caleb the
son of Jephunneh the Kenezite unto this day, because
that he wholly followed the LORD God of Israel.
(Josh. 14:6-14)

Caleb said, "In the past I followed the Lord God." What
was he talking about? He and Joshua were the spies under
Moses who years earlier had believed God's promises.
While the rest of the spies had said, "We are afraid," and
had turned the people aside, Caleb and Joshua had said,
"We can take the land because God says we can."

When the campaigns had broken the heart of the land,
Caleb (now 85) came to Joshua and said, "Now by faith I'm
going to do what I said all along could be done." What a
man! Here he was, out of step among a people who, for the
sake of peace and wealth, were not continuing the warfare.
In that moment, as in the past, Caleb followed the Lord.
Caleb actually went up and claimed his land—fought for it
and won it (Josh. 15:13-19)—and proved what he had believed for many long years. Apparently the city he captured

was one of the great fortresses. When the spies had seen it, they thought it would be extremely difficult to take; but Caleb had maintained, "We can take it under God." Now he proved this by faith. This was Caleb!

Caleb was not following a new principle. This was the principle of his life. When he was a spy, he was faithful to God, saying the conquest could be achieved. Under Joshua, we can be sure, he continued in battle with confidence. When the heart of the land was broken, he reaffirmed his principle of trusting God by not turning aside into these other cul-de-sacs. So a section of the promised land fell into Caleb's hands while the others were sitting in the midst of peace and tribute and not possessing the promises of God.

Promises to Christians

Caleb's faithfulness speaks to us today. If you and I have cast ourselves upon Christ, if we have believed in him in the biblical way, if we have been justified, the central battle has been won, just as when the Israelites' southern and northern campaigns broke the heart of the resistance. But there are also promises made to Christians. We are called upon to *possess our possessions.* Was God, who gave the people the power to break the strongholds, not able to give them the possessions? Was God's power ended? If we are Christians, we have believed that Christ in the infinite value of his death takes away our guilt and opens the way to God for us. Has Christ lost his power since we were justified? Have God's promises to us diminished?

What are God's promises to Christians? We could follow several veins, but I would like to follow this one: the promises of the fruit and power of the Holy Spirit. As Jesus was preparing to leave his disciples, he promised, "I will not leave you orphans. I will come to you" (John 14:18). Here is the promise of God: "I am going to send the Holy Spirit, the third Person of the Trinity, to live within every true Christian from Pentecost on." Romans 8 emphasizes that the Holy Spirit is the agent through which the power of the victorious, resurrected Christ brings forth fruit in a Christian's life.

Christ has not left us orphans. The Holy Spirit dwells within us. And this fact has great implications. Jesus promised his followers, "But ye shall receive power [from the same Greek word which gives us our word *dynamite*], after that the Holy Ghost is come upon you: and ye shall be witnesses unto me both in Jerusalem, and in all Judea, and in Samaria, and unto the uttermost part of the earth" (Acts 1: 8). The Holy Spirit will be Christ's agent in us—producing dynamite power so we can witness to this rebellious world.

The Holy Spirit also gives us the fruit of the Spirit, which is described in Galatians: "But the fruit of the Spirit is love, joy, peace, longsuffering, gentleness, goodness, faith, meekness, temperance: against such there is no law. And they that are Christ's have crucified the flesh with the affections and lusts. If we live in the Spirit, let us also walk in the Spirit" (Gal. 5:22-25). If we have accepted Christ as our Savior, we are indwelt by the Holy Spirit. Isn't that fine? All right, then, let us walk in the Spirit. Let us possess our possessions.

What was the Israelites' trouble? Why did they not possess their possessions? Very simple: They wanted their peace and materialism. These things always stand in the way of the people of God. There is an intriguing parallel in the parable of the sower: "And that which fell among thorns are they, which, when they have heard, go forth, and are choked with cares and riches and pleasures of this life, and bring no fruit to perfection" (Lk. 8:14). There are people who hear the gospel and turn away because of the cares of life, and there are people who turn away because of their fears of losing riches and pleasure. But Christians, too, can be so caught up in the cares and riches and pleasures of this world that they bring no fruit to perfection.

What Jesus desires is this: "That on the good ground are

they, which in an honest and good heart, having heard the word, keep it, and bring forth fruit with patience" (Lk. 8:15). Hold it fast! Hold it fast! Bring forth fruit with patience! Patience in what? First, patience in enduring the cares of this world and the trouble that Christianity brings. Does Christianity bring you any troubles? If it does not, you have not been active enough. As Christians we are in the midst of war. If we never have any troubles, if we have nothing but peace, we have not been involved in this war in the midst of a generation that has rebelled against God. Second, we need patience in resisting the riches and pleasures which can also stop fruit-bearing.

What was the first reason why the Israelites did not possess their possessions? They wanted peace. Doesn't this exactly parallel the "cares"? What was the second reason? They wanted tribute. Because of riches and pleasures, a Christian can also be distracted from continuing God's conquest. That which stood in the way of blessing in the time of Joshua is exactly what today stands in the way of a Christian's bearing fruit.

With the Israelites, the master conquest was over. With us the master conquest ended at two great historic points: a cross in space and time (where Jesus said, "It is finished"— the propitiatory work was complete) and the moment we personally were justified (when God, the Judge of all the universe, declared, "Your guilt is gone. You are returned to me").

Back in Joshua's day when the master conquest was over God was the same, his promise was the same, his power was the same. But the people did not possess their possessions because of their desire for peace and for tribute. We Christians stand in the same danger. It is all too easy to fail to possess the possessions God has promised because we either draw back out of fear of the troubles that being a Christian will bring us or we become caught up in the affluent society where people sail their little boats upon this plastic culture.

ten
East and West
of Jordan

After the three successful campaigns, God commanded the children of Israel to divide the land in faith even before it was completely conquered. "Only divide it by lot unto the Israelites for an inheritance, as I have commanded thee," he said (Josh. 13:6). Jacob, of course, had twelve sons. And God had made a covenant with Abraham, Isaac and Jacob that all twelve would have an inheritance in the land of promise.

The land was divided in three steps. The first took place under Moses on the east side of Jordan, the second and third under Joshua on the west side, first at Gilgal, then at Shiloh. Moses gave two and a half tribes—Reuben, Gad and a half-tribe of Manasseh—an inheritance on the eastern side of the Jordan before he died. After the major campaigns, Joshua divided the land west of the Jordan among the remaining tribes. As we shall study later, the Levites received no land as a capital possession, though they were given land to live in.

Joshua 13:15-31 reminds us of the inheritances received on the east side of Jordan and then Joshua 13:32 summarizes, "These are the countries [the portions of the land] which Moses did distribute for an inheritance in the plains of Moab, on the other side of Jordan, by Jericho, eastward."

The final verse of Joshua 13 reminds us that Levi did not receive a normal share of the land because the Levites would live on the sacrifices: "But unto the tribe of Levi Moses gave not any inheritance: the LORD God of Israel was their inheritance, as he [God] said unto them." The Levites did not receive any land because Moses had said so, and Moses said so because the Lord God of Israel had said so. Thus Joshua 13 also emphasizes that the Pentateuch was already completely normative. It was the Word of God to these people. Was this because Moses was a great or wise man? Not at all. It was because Moses was the mouthpiece of God. The Levites received no land because of a propositional statement which called forth a specific action in history.

Joshua 14 describes the beginning of the division of the land on the west side of Jordan. The people were at Gilgal, which had remained their central camp throughout the warfare. There the second phase of the allotment occurred: "And these are the countries which the children of Israel inherited in the land of Canaan, which Eleazar the priest, and Joshua the son of Nun, and the heads of the fathers of the tribes of the children of Israel, distributed for inheritance to them. By lot was their inheritance, as the LORD commanded by the hand of Moses, for the nine tribes, and for the half tribe" (Josh. 14:1-2). Who oversaw the distribution? The priests, Joshua and the elders. How were the portions determined? By lot. So it was God who made the division. The men only supervised the distribution under the hand of God through the lot.

The Division to Judah

First on the west side of the Jordan, land was given to Judah. Caleb was of Judah, and so his act of faith is discussed in the second half of Joshua 14. Then Joshua 15:1-12 tells us the boundaries of Judah's territory. This portion began at the shore of the Dead Sea and ended at the river of Egypt (not the Nile, but a little wadi, Wadi el Arish), that is, at the bend of the Mediterranean between Palestine and Egypt. This area contained Jerusalem, which became important as David's city and the capital of the southern kingdom. Verses 20-63 provide a detailed list of the cities and towns in Judah's inheritance.

Why did Judah, who was not the oldest son, receive the first of the land on the west side of the Jordan? You must remember the continuity of history and the continuity of prophecy which are interwoven in the Scripture. God knows and God sometimes tells the future. As a matter of fact, Isaiah and other writers insist that this knowledge is one of the marks which distinguishes God from other gods. Because he is a living, infinite God, and not just an idol or a projection of man's mind, he can tell us the future course of history, just as we can read a history of the past.

Long before the land was divided, the dying Jacob gave a prophecy (Gen. 49). It is sometimes called a blessing, but it was really a foretelling about Jacob's sons.

Jacob spoke first of all to Reuben, the first-born, the one who should have had pre-eminence: "Reuben, thou art my firstborn, my might, and the beginning of my strength, the excellency of dignity, and the excellency of power: unstable as water, thou shalt not excel; because thou wentest up to thy father's bed; then defiledst thou it: he went up to my couch" (Gen. 49:3-4). What had Reuben done? This boy, growing into manhood, had had sexual relations with Bilah, his father's concubine (Gen. 35:22). Because of this, Jacob set aside his pre-eminence.

The next two sons were Simeon and Levi. Jacob dealt with them like this:

Simeon and Levi are brethren; instruments of cruelty [swords of violence] are in their habitations. O my soul,

165

come not thou into their secret; unto their assembly,
mine honour, be not thou united: for in their anger
they slew a man, and in their selfwill they digged down
a wall. Cursed be their anger, for it was fierce; and
their wrath, for it was cruel: I will divide them in Jacob,
and scatter them in Israel. (Gen. 49:5-7)

This prophecy referred to an incident which had involved
Shechem, a prince in a neighboring land, and Dinah, a
daughter of Jacob (Gen. 34). Shechem found Dinah in the
field, had sexual relations with her and then wanted to mar-
ry her. These two boys, Simeon and Levi, through a strategy which included a colossal lie, weakened Shechem's
whole people and then killed them all. Because the brothers
had lied, Jacob isolated himself from their act; and because
of their act, they were not going to receive the first place
either. Rather, they were to be scattered. They were not to
have a fixed location like the rest of the tribes.

This has a lot to say, does it not, to the existential mentality that history is going nowhere. The biblical emphasis is
constantly the reverse: History does have meaning; the past
brings forth the present and the present influences the
future. Something happens in history because of a previous
effect. Hume was wrong. Cause-and-effect does exist, not
only in science but in meaningful, significant human
events.

Jacob prophesied that Simeon and Levi were to be scattered in the land. Something happened, however, to modi-
fy this. The prophecy was still fulfilled, yet it was divided
into two halves. It stood as Jacob had given it concerning
Simeon, but it shifted in the case of Levi. In the midst of the
orgies around the golden calf, Moses gave a call: Who is on
the Lord's side? Who will speak for God? Who will act for
God against a rebellious people? Then "all the sons of Levi
gathered themselves together unto him" (Ex. 32:26) and
went forward to end this revolt. Therefore, though the
scattering stood, it was turned into a blessing. The Levites,

along with the descendants of Aaron (who were of the tribe of Levi), were given a special closeness to the altar and to the Jewish worship.

Now we know why Judah received his place first in the giving of the land on the west of the Jordan, the heart of the promised land. Reuben, Levi and Simeon had all been set aside.

Jacob continued his prophecy by turning to Judah:

Judah, thou art he whom thy brethren shall praise: thy hand shall be in the neck of thine enemies; thy father's children shall bow down before thee. Judah is a lion's whelp: from the prey, my son, thou art gone up: he stooped down, he couched as a lion, and as an old lion; who shall rouse him up? The sceptre shall not depart from Judah, nor a staff [or lawgiver] from between his feet, until Shiloh come; and unto him shall the gathering of the peoples be. (Gen. 49:8-10)

So Judah was awarded the pre-eminence among the people of God. Judah received the first share of the land on the west of the river, which included Jerusalem. This is important because Judah is the one out of whom David comes, and David is the one out of whom the truly great Ruler, Christ, comes.

The emphasis in Jacob's prophecy was that Judah would rule, and, whether one translates the word in verse 10 as "lawgiver" or "staff," this emphasis is not changed. In Judges 5:14 the word is used to mean "a ruler" who symbolizes his authority by holding a sceptre. In other words, in Genesis 49:10 a double emphasis is being given through the parallel meaning of the words, *sceptre* and *staff*.

David, Solomon and their successors came as partial fulfillment of this prophecy that Judah would rule, but the whole truth is far deeper. A greater reign was being prophesied here than the secular regimes of the later Jewish kings. Jacob spoke of Judah as a lion, and in Revelation this symbol is applied to one special Person: "One of the elders saith unto me, Weep not; behold the Lion of the tribe of Juda, the Root of David, hath prevailed to open the book [of redemption], and to loose the seven seals thereof" (Rev. 5:5). The final rule that Jacob was describing was the rule of Christ, who shall be the great King of Israel as well as its redeemer.

Numbers 21:18 speaks of Moses as "the lawgiver" or "staff" or "sceptre." Deuteronomy describes Moses as a "prophet" and records Moses' great prophecy about the coming Messiah: "The LORD thy God will raise up unto thee a Prophet from the midst of thee, of thy brethren, like unto me; unto him ye shall hearken" (Deut. 18:15). As we have seen, the New Testament expressly relates this to Christ. The idea of the ruler has shifted from Levi (Moses) to Judah (Christ)—an important change. Moses was "the lawgiver" or "ruler," but a time would come when the ruler would not be from the tribe of Levi but from the tribe of Judah, just as the great prophet when he would come would not come from Levi but from Judah. Interestingly, the last phrase of Psalm 60:7 uses the same word: Judah is my sceptre or ruler.

Also in Jacob's prophecy we find the term *Shiloh*. When the southern kingdom's rebellion against God came to the full and the kingly line from Solomon became totally corrupt, God made a striking statement through the prophet Ezekiel:

And thou, profane wicked prince of Israel, whose day is come, when iniquity shall have an end, thus saith the Lord GOD; Remove the diadem, and take off the crown: this shall not be the same: exalt him that is low, and abase him that is high. I will overturn, overturn, overturn, it: and it shall be no more, until he come whose right it is; and I will give it him. (Ezek. 21:25-27)

"I'm done with you!" God said. "But I'm not done totally because somebody is going to come—somebody 'whose right it is'—and then he will rule." Some believe *Shiloh* means "The Coming One." One was coming who was going to be the real ruler of the Jews.

It is important that the division of the land occurred by the God-directed lot and not by the wisdom of men. Joshua and the other Jewish leaders did not read the prophecy and then deliberately fulfill it. God fulfilled it through the throwing of the lot. He guided the lot because Christ would fulfill all of Jacob's prophecy: He, the lion of Judah, would come to be Israel's ruler.

Who is this Christ, this King of the Jews? The Gospel of John portrays the Coming One for us. At the beginning of Jesus' ministry, Nathanael identified him: "Rabbi, thou art the Son of God; thou art the King of Israel" (John 1:49). Here was a double emphasis: Jesus is deity but he is also the Old Testament-prophesied King. In Matthew, the wise men came asking, "Where is he that is born King of the Jews?" (Mt. 2:2). They asked this of Herod, who was king of the Jews by the grace of Caesar, and his wrath was stirred up because he was threatened by Christ's kingship. In Luke, Christ's kingship was strikingly proclaimed at his triumphal entry. As Jesus rode into Jerusalem just before his death, the people strewed his path with palm branches and with their clothes, saying, "Blessed be the King that cometh in the name of the Lord" (Lk. 19:38).

This same Jesus is coming again in a space-time moment future to us. Just as Joshua stood in judgment against the Amorites when their iniquity was full, Jesus will come in flaming judgment on the world when the iniquity of the era of the Gentiles is full. What is his name? "KING OF KINGS, AND LORD OF LORDS" (Rev. 19:16).

Jacob prophesied finally that "unto him shall the gathering of the peoples be" (Gen. 49:10). This is one of the many Old Testament prophecies that say that the Gentiles will have a place among the people of God. The Coming One is not only the King of the Jews but also the Gatherer of the Peoples. And those of us who are Gentiles redeemed by the work of Christ are part of the fulfillment of that prophecy.

The Division to Joseph

After the division to Judah came the division to Joseph (Josh. 16:1—17:18). Joseph had two sons, Manasseh and Ephraim, and each son's tribe was given a share. Though Ephraim was the younger, he received his place in the giving of the land on the west of Jordan before Manasseh. Why? Once more prophecy entered in:

And Israel [Jacob] said unto Joseph, I had not thought to see thy face: and, lo, God hath shewed me also thy seed. And Joseph brought them out from between his knees, and he bowed himself with his face to the earth. And Joseph took them both, Ephraim in his right hand toward Israel's left hand, and Manasseh in his left hand toward Israel's right hand, and brought them near unto him. And Israel stretched out his right hand, and laid it upon Ephraim's head, who was the younger, and his left hand upon Manasseh's head, guiding his hands wittingly; for Manasseh was the firstborn. And he blessed Joseph, and said, God, before whom my fathers Abraham and Isaac did walk, the God which fed me all my life long unto this day, the angel which redeemed me from all evil, bless the lads; and let my name be named on them, and the name of my fathers Abraham and Isaac; and let them grow into a multitude in the midst of the earth.

And when Joseph saw that his father laid his right hand upon the head of Ephraim, it displeased him: and he held up his father's hand, to remove it from Ephraim's head unto Manasseh's head. And Joseph said unto his father, Not so, my father: for this is the firstborn; put thy right hand upon his head. And his father refused, and said, I know it, my son, I know it: he also shall become a people, and he also shall be great: but truly his younger brother shall be greater

than he, and his seed shall become a multitude of nations. And he blessed them that day, saying, In thee
shall Israel bless, saying, God make thee as Ephraim
and as Manasseh: and he set Ephraim before Manasseh. (Gen. 48:11-20)

God, working through the lot, preserved the continuity of
this prophecy given all those long years previously.

After Ephraim was given his place, the half-tribe of
Manasseh that had not received land on the east side of the
Jordan was allotted its inheritance. Usually the land was
given to sons, but in this case daughters also received it because there were no sons (Josh. 17:3-4). Once more we are
reminded that these people regarded the Pentateuch as
normative in every detail, for when the women presented
their case they argued, "The LORD commanded Moses to
give us an inheritance among our brethren. Therefore according to the commandment of the LORD he gave them
an inheritance among the brethren of their father" (Josh.
17:4). They regarded the Pentateuch as the Word of God
and as something which not only conveyed some sort of religious feeling but also gave specific commands which were
to be obeyed in detail. They were referring to Numbers
27:1-11 and to Numbers 36.

The Final Divisions at Shiloh

Prior to the final divisions of the land, the Israelites moved
permanently from Gilgal to Shiloh (Josh. 18:1). Shiloh was
in the hill country, just off the highway to the north of Beth-
el and Ai as one travels toward Gerizim and Ebal. The Israelites left the plain and established themselves in the
mountains. They took the tabernacle with them, which
means they removed everything from their former camp.

Although the big campaigns were finished, much land
remained to be taken. Therefore, they sent spies to map out
the territory so that the lot could be thrown for this piece of
geography. "And the men went and passed through the

land, and described it by cities into seven parts in a book, and came again to Joshua to the host at Shiloh" (Josh. 18:9). Writing was so common that the spies were able to write their report and present it to Joshua.

The fall of the lot located Benjamin right next to Judah: "And the lot of the tribe of the children of Benjamin came up according to their families: and the coast of their lot came forth between the children of Judah and the children of Joseph" (Josh. 18:11). As a matter of fact, their land came together at the city of Jerusalem. Moses had made this prophecy concerning Benjamin: "The beloved of the LORD shall dwell in safety by him; and the LORD shall cover him all the day long, and he shall dwell between his shoulders" (Deut. 33:12). Benjamin was going to have a special closeness to the Lord. When the northern tribes later turned away from God, the tribes that stood fast were Judah and Benjamin; so Moses' prophecy was fulfilled.

In the second lot thrown at Shiloh, the remaining tribes received their land. Simeon did not receive a separate inheritance because, as you remember, Jacob said he was going to be scattered. He was given a place in the midst of Judah. So while in the fulfilling of the prophecy of Genesis 49:5-7 the Levites became the special servants of God scattered throughout the people, the Simeonites had no real share of the land.

Next, Zebulun's place was designated. Jacob had prophesied concerning Zebulun: "Zebulun shall dwell at the haven of the sea; and he shall be for an haven of ships" (Gen. 49:13). He was the only person related to seafaring. And when the land was divided, Zebulun's "border went up toward the sea" (Josh. 19:11).

Places were designated, too, for Issachar (Josh. 19:17), Asher (Josh. 19:24), Naphtali (Josh. 19:32) and Dan (Josh. 19:40). Finally, Joshua was given a special inheritance, the city of Timnath-serah. Every tribe now had its land. The divisions were complete. The entire matter is summarized like this: "These are the inheritances, which Eleazar the priest, and Joshua the son of Nun, and the heads of the fathers of the tribes of the children of Israel, divided for an inheritance by lot in Shiloh before the LORD, at the door of the tabernacle of the congregation. So they made an end of dividing the country" (Josh. 19:51).

The Conclusion of the Era of Conquest

We need to look at one more chapter, Joshua 22, in order to bring the era of the campaigns to a close.

When the two and a half tribes were given their land east of the Jordan, Moses said to them, "The west side still has to be taken. Are you going to stay here in peace while your brothers who fought for you have to go on in war?"

The fighting men from these tribes responded, "We'll go with the rest and fight as long as the war is on."

To which Moses replied, "Good. Then all is well."

These men built cities and left some of their people on their land. This means that for the seven years of campaign these soldiers were separated from their wives, their families, their inheritance. Now that the campaigns were over and the land divided it was time to go home:

Then Joshua called the Reubenites, and the Gadites, and the half tribe of Manasseh, and said unto them, Ye have kept all that Moses the servant of the LORD commanded you, and have obeyed my voice in all that I commanded you: ye have not left your brethren these many days unto this day, but have kept the charge of the commandment of the LORD your God. And now the LORD your God hath given rest unto your brethren, as he promised them: therefore now return ye, and get you unto your tents, and unto the land of your possession, which Moses the servant of the LORD gave you on the other side Jordan. But take diligent heed to do the commandment and the law, which Moses the servant of the LORD charged you, to love the LORD

your God, and to walk in all his ways, and to keep his
commandments, and to cleave unto him, and to serve
him with all your heart and with all your soul. So Joshua blessed them, and sent them away: and they went
unto their tents. (Josh. 22:1-6)

If we use a little imagination, we can feel the tremendous
emotion involved in the parting of these comrades at arms.
We can picture the men going through the camp, finding
the friends with whom they had fought side by side and saying goodby to some who had even saved their lives. They
shook hands and they parted, as worshipers of God, as
friends and as fellow companions in war. There is a com-
radeship among men in titanic moments that is one of the
great "mystiques" of life. It is the explanation of the mys-
tique of the rope—two men on a mountain battling nature
together, depending for their very lives on a common rope.

As the comrades left, they took with them much spoil.
Joshua commanded them to divide the spoil with those who
had remained on the east side to guard the possessions
(Josh. 22:8). Then "the children of Reuben and the children of Gad and the half tribe of Manasseh returned, and
departed from the children of Israel out of Shiloh, which
is in the land of Canaan" (Josh. 22:9).

The men of the two and a half tribes traveled east and put
the Jordan between themselves and the majority of the
people. Then came a new note: "And when they came unto
the borders of Jordan, that are in the land of Canaan, the
children of Reuben and the children of Gad and the half
tribe of Manasseh built there an altar by Jordan, a great
altar to see to" (Josh. 22:10). They built a huge altar, one
that could be seen a long way off. And suddenly the com-
plexion of the situation changed. The men who were with
Joshua and the priests on the west side of the river spread
the word through the camp, "The people who have left us
have built a new altar! They've built a new altar!" You can
hear this bubbling through the camp. The men with whom

they had been shaking hands just a few days before seemed to be establishing a rival worship. And these people said, "Something must be done about this! This is rebellion against God!"

Joshua 22:12 is one of the most touching verses we will ever find, if we do not just read it as words but see the human content in it: "And when the children of Israel heard of it, the whole congregation of the children of Israel gathered themselves together at Shiloh, to go up to war against them." That is just terrific! We ought to play the bagpipes! These men had just parted as companions in war. I do not know whether they shook hands as we do or rubbed noses like the Eskimos or, like the Brazilians, slapped each other on the back until they could not breathe any longer, but, whichever it was, they said goodby in the strongest, heartiest sense imaginable. But now they thought the holiness of God was being threatened. So these men, who were sick of war, said, "The holiness of God demands no compromise." I would to God that the church of the twentieth century would learn this lesson. The holiness of the God who exists demands that there be no compromise in the area of truth. Tears? I am sure there were tears, but there had to be battle if there was rebellion against God.

The leaders on the west side did their best, however, to straighten the matter out. They did not go off to war without first attempting reconciliation. This is a good example of the simultaneous exhibition of both the holiness and the love of God. It is a biblical example of truth and beauty. Because of their concern for God's holiness, they were ready for battle; but the fact that they did not attack immediately was a practical demonstration of love. Instead, they chose a prince from each of the tribes and sent them along with Phinehas the high priest to see if this matter could be straightened out. When they confronted the two and a half tribes on the east, they did not beat around the bush. I am convinced that what we see here is the kind of thing that

175

Jesus later commanded concerning a practical relationship among the people of God. They came without compromise, talked face to face and made an honest charge:

> And they came unto the children of Reuben, and to the children of Gad, and to the half tribe of Manasseh, unto the land of Gilead, and they spake with them, saying, Thus saith the whole congregation of the LORD, What trespass is this that ye have committed against the God of Israel, to turn away this day from following the LORD, in that ye have builded you an altar, that ye might rebel this day against the LORD? Is the iniquity of Peor too little for us, from which we are not cleansed until this day, although there was a plague in the congregation of the LORD, but that ye must turn away this day from following the LORD? and it will be, seeing ye rebel to day against the LORD, that to morrow he will be wroth with the whole congregation of Israel. Notwithstanding, if the land of your possession be unclean, then pass ye over unto the land of the possession of the LORD, wherein the LORD's tabernacle dwelleth, and take possession among us: but rebel not against the LORD, nor rebel against us, in building you an altar beside the altar of the LORD our God. Did not Achan the son of Zerah commit a trespass in the accursed thing, and wrath fell on all the congregation of Israel? and that man perished not alone in his iniquity. (Josh. 22:15-20)

Notice that the whole congregation agreed with the charges. This was not a political issue, the two and a half tribes talking rebellion against the rest. Rebellion against God was the issue. The representatives reminded the others of the seriousness of this, not only for the people who had sinned but for all the people of God. They reminded them of the iniquity of Peor, which was a corporate sin that had occurred approximately eight years before. (See Num. 25:1-3, 18.) They said, "Because the people of the congregation were involved, everybody suffered" (Josh. 22:18). And they reminded them of what happened when Achan sinned. They said, "You can't sin with impunity and the people of God not be injured. When either a group or one man sins, the whole people is injured. Consequently, we are here to prevent that." This illustrates the practicality of love. It is no use talking about love if there is no action to it. What was the practicality in this case? It was shown in the willingness of the tribes west of the Jordan to sacrifice money and land to resolve the situation properly.

Once more, here is the tragedy of the modern church: Our spirituality and our brotherhood often stop at the point of material possessions. In the early church this was not so. The Christians had things in common not because there was a law to this effect, not because this was an enforced Marx-Engels communism, but because they loved each other. And a love that does not go down into the practical stuff of life, including money and possessions, is absolute junk! To think that love is talking softly rather than saying something sharply and that it is not carried down into the practical stuff of life is not biblical. We must say with tears that the orthodox evangelical church in our generation has been poor at this point.

This generation of Jews was not. They were willing to go to battle, but they were dialoguing in love to try to find a solution. The solution even came to this: "If you don't want to live over here, bring everything into our land. Bring your herds, bring your sheep. We'll move over in our pasture lands. We'll move out of the villages. We'll give you some of the cities. You can share it with us, but don't rebel against God." How many would have come? Probably the total number who had entered the land had been about two and a half million. Thus those on the east side of Jordan would have been many, many thousand. What a practical lesson for the people of God—a generous, loving offer was made at material cost!

The people being confronted could have gotten angry
and responded, "What are you getting so worked up for?"
But they did not. We see here the interplay that should
characterize discipline in the church of Christ. The majority thought a trespass had been committed. They did not
gloss it over; indeed, they were ready to go to battle in order
to preserve the holiness and the commands of God. In reply, the other side did not just stalk out of the church door,
as it were. They gave an honest, open answer:

Then the children of Reuben and the children of Gad
and the half tribe of Manasseh answered, and said unto the heads of the thousands of Israel, The LORD
God of gods, the LORD God of gods, he knoweth, and
Israel he shall know; if it be in rebellion, or if in trans-
gression against the LORD, (save us not this day,) that
we have built us an altar to turn from following the
LORD, or if to offer thereon burnt-offering or meat-
offering, or if to offer peace-offerings thereon, let
the LORD himself require it; and if we have not rather
done it for fear of this thing, saying, In time to come
your children might speak unto our children, saying,
What have ye to do with the LORD God of Israel? For
the LORD hath made Jordan a border between us and
you, ye children of Reuben and children of Gad; ye
have no part in the LORD: so shall your children make
our children cease from fearing the LORD. Therefore
we said, Let us now prepare to build us an altar, not for
burnt-offering, nor for sacrifice: but that it may be a
witness between us, and you, and our generations after
us, that we might do the service of the LORD before
him with our burnt-offerings, and with our sacrifices,
and with our peace-offerings; that your children may
not say to our children in time to come, Ye have no part
in the LORD. Therefore said we, that it shall be, when
they should so say to us or to our generations in time to
come, that we may say again, Behold the pattern of the

altar of the LORD, which our fathers made, not for burnt-offerings, nor for sacrifices; but it is a witness between us and you. God forbid that we should rebel against the LORD, and turn this day from following the LORD, to build an altar for burnt-offerings, for meat-offerings, or for sacrifices, beside the altar of the LORD our God that is before his tabernacle. (Josh. 22:21-29)

I love this: "We know in our hearts right now that God is satisfied; and we are going to tell you the facts, and we know you will then be satisfied." They did not have to convince God. God already knew. But they were going to point out the situation lovingly so that the rest of the people of God would know.

This statement, it seems to me, is the key: "If it be in rebellion, or if in trespass against the LORD, save us not this day." They agreed that if they were worshiping another god or rebelling against God and his commands (including the commands about how to worship), they deserved judgment. This is the basis of the marvelous results which we will see shortly. These results were rooted and grounded in an agreement that God is holy, that God's commands must not be breached and that if God's commands are breached this deserves judgment. There was no accommodation of relativism, no Hegelian synthesis, no compromise with truth. The reason these people were able to have a real unity and a real peace was that they were locked into the truth and commandments of God. Without the concept that is laid down here, any right unity is impossible. Any unity, any peace, that is not rooted in truth is nothing!

The two and a half tribes protested that their action was not sinful. They did not build this altar for the purpose of rebellion, nor even for the purpose of worship. Why then did they build it? They intended it to be a pattern, a replica, of the true altar by the tabernacle. They wanted this large copy of the real altar to stand as a witness that they, too, had a right to cross the Jordan and worship.

So we come to the marvelous conclusion:

And when Phinehas the priest, and the princes of the congregation and heads of the thousands of Israel which were with him, heard the words that the children of Reuben and the children of Gad and the children of Manasseh spake, it pleased them. And Phinehas the son of Eleazar the priest said unto the children of Reuben, and to the children of Gad, and to the children of Manasseh, This day we perceive that the LORD is among us, because ye have not committed this trespass against the LORD: now ye have delivered the children of Israel out of the hand of the LORD. And Phinehas the son of Eleazar the priest, and the princes, returned from the children of Reuben, and from the children of Gad, out of the land of Gilead, unto the land of Canaan, to the children of Israel, and brought them word again. And the thing pleased the children of Israel; and the children of Israel blessed God, and did not intend to go up against them in battle, to destroy the land wherein the children of Reuben and Gad dwelt. And the children of Reuben and the children of Gad called the altar Ed: for it shall be a witness between us that the LORD is God. (Josh. 22:30-34)

First, the ten princes from the west of Jordan along with Phinehas the priest turned to the rest and said, "We're agreed. It's tremendous! Everything is in place. We see there is no rebellion here. We give you the right hand of fellowship." Then they returned to the other side of the Jordan and reported to the remainder of the people. The land was at peace, and there was a happy ending indeed. On both sides of the river, the witness of this altar stood, and as it were there came a cry from the entire people of God, "The Lord he is God! The Lord he is God!"

Why was there this happy ending? Because of the two steps I have mentioned. First, there was a clear agreement on the importance of doctrine and truth, an understanding that the holiness of God demands bowing before him and obeying his commands. Remember Joshua's words as he sent the people away to the other side of the Jordan: "Take diligent heed . . . to love the LORD your God, and to walk in all his ways, and to keep his commandments." There was a happy ending because the people did this.

Second, those who were courageous in standing for truth were also courageous in acting in love. If there had only been a stand for truth, there would never have been a happy ending. There would have only been war because the ten tribes would have torn across the river and killed the other Israelites without talking to anybody. There would have been sadness in the midst of misunderstanding. But because of the love of God, the tribes talked to each other openly, and the love and holiness of God were able to come together. Psalm 85 speaks of the righteousness of God and the love of God kissing each other (v. 10). This was what happened here.

What is a Christian's duty in life? He has only one basic duty: to exhibit the existence of God and to exhibit his character in the midst of a rebellious world. What is the character of God? God is holy and God is love. Christians—both individually and corporately—have a duty to stand for God's truth with no compromise while simultaneously dealing in love with brothers and sisters in Christ—yes, and with men and women outside the church. Joshua 22 is not just history; it is a rule in the continuity of God's commands to his people through the flow of history. It is an example for the people of God in dealing with each other for all time.

This chapter has emphasized two things: (1) the continuity of prophecy in the flow of history (the very opposite of modern man's not being able to tell the difference between fantasy and reality) and (2) the importance of right action among the people of God. When the people of God are acting as they should, they manifest the unity of the holiness and the love of God.

Whenever church leaders ask us to choose between the holiness of God and the love of God, we must refuse. For when the love of God becomes compromised, it is not the love of God. When the holiness of God becomes hardness and a lack of beauty, it is not the holiness of God. This is the calling to us who live in the New Testament era too—to practice the holiness and love of God with no compromise to either. If anything, it is an even greater responsibility for us than for those who practiced it so beautifully in Joshua's time, for we live on this side of the cross, the open tomb, the ascension and Pentecost.

eleven
The Cities of Refuge

As we have seen, the Levites were given special cities scattered throughout the other tribes' portions. It was at Shiloh that the Levites came forward to claim that inheritance, referring, as we have seen the Jews so frequently do, to the Pentateuch as an authoritative canon which should be consciously obeyed.

> Then came near the heads of the fathers of the Levites unto Eleazar the priest, and unto Joshua the son of Nun, and unto the heads of the fathers of the tribes of the children of Israel; and they spake unto them at Shiloh in the land of Canaan, saying, The LORD commanded by the hand of Moses to give us cities to dwell in, with the suburbs thereof for our cattle. And the children of Israel gave unto the Levites out of their inheritance, at the commandment of the LORD, these cities and their suburbs. (Josh. 21:1-3)

Numbers 35 records the command to which the Levites referred Eleazar and Joshua:

> And the LORD spake unto Moses in the plains of

Moab by Jordan near Jericho, saying, Command the children of Israel, that they give unto the Levites of the inheritance of their possession cities to dwell in; and ye shall give also unto the Levites suburbs for the cities round about them. And the cities shall they have to dwell in: and the suburbs of them shall be for their cattle, and for their goods, and for all their beasts. (Num. 35:1-3)

Moses himself followed this command when he was dividing the land on the east side of the Jordan: "Only unto the tribe of Levi he gave none inheritance; the sacrifices of the LORD God of Israel made by fire are their inheritance, as he said unto them" (Josh. 13:14; see also v. 33). Speaking of the division of the land at Shiloh, Joshua said, "But the Levites have no part among you; for the priesthood of the LORD is their inheritance" (Josh. 18:7). God had spoken: The Levites were to be a special case.

We saw that Simeon and Levi were given no normal inheritance because of their sin. Simeon was scattered in the midst of Judah. On the other hand, Levi's faithfulness at the time of the golden calf turned his scattering from a confusion into a blessing. At that moment, the Levites became the servants of God. They had no separate territory, but they had cities throughout the land.

The Levites' allotment, of course, raises a question. Men need not only a place to live but also food to eat. The economy of the Israelites was rooted in agriculture, which meant that land was crucial. Having land gave a person his basic economic possibilities. The Levites, therefore, had no such possibilities because while they had villages, they did not have an extensive territory upon which to grow crops or raise sheep and cattle. Where were they going to get their food? The answer is that they did not need a regular portion because they were to receive the tithes of the rest of the Jews. While other people had large territories for sheep, cows or grain as a pay crop, the basic income for the Levites was the tithes which the others gave. When the Lord said to Aaron, "Thou shalt have no inheritance in their land, neither shalt thou have any part among them: I am thy part and thine inheritance among the children of Israel" (Num. 18:20), he did not mean that Aaron was only to stand in a special relationship to him but that Aaron and the Levites were to be recipients of the gifts made to God. God commanded, "Thus speak unto the Levites, and say unto them, When ye take of the children of Israel the tithe which I have given you from them for your inheritance, then ye shall offer up an heave-offering of it for the LORD, even a tenth part of the tithe" (Num. 18:26). The Levites' tithes were then passed on to Aaron and the other priests (Num. 18:28). It was a double tithe: The people tithed and gave to the Levites, and the Levites tithed and gave to the priests.

This continuity of the tithe, which began at least with Abraham and continued in the story of Jericho, Achan and Ai, came down to the Israelites in the land and the command of proportional giving passed on eventually into the New Testament. Paul wrote to the Corinthian Christians, "Upon the first day of the week let every one of you lay by him in store, as God hath prospered him" (1 Cor. 16:2). So the command to the church is the same as the command to God's people in the Old Testament—proportional giving. Giving to God proportionately is not optional. God specifically commands it.

The Distribution of the Levites' Cities

How were the Levites' cities distributed? The distribution was based on the fact that Levi, the son of Jacob, had three sons: Gershon, Kohath and Merari (Gen. 46:11). Each of the sons was consistently dealt with as a unit throughout the centuries that followed. For example, when the people made camp during the wilderness wanderings the Levites were always divided into three sections. The Gershonites pitched their tents "behind the tabernacle westward"

(Num. 3:23), and this one family had a special task: "And the charge of the sons of Gershon in the tabernacle of the congregation shall be the tabernacle, and the tent, the covering thereof, and the hanging for the door of the tabernacle of the congregation, and the hangings of the court, and the curtain for the door of the court, which is by the tabernacle, and by the altar round about, and the cords of it for all the service thereof " (Josh. 3:25-26). In other words, they had charge of the tent itself. When the Israelites broke camp, the Gershonites carried this material with them. The family of Kohath pitched "on the side of the tabernacle southward" (Num. 3:29). They, too, had a special task: They dealt with all the instruments of worship that were used outside the Holy of Holies (Num. 3:31). (The priests themselves took care of the instruments of worship within the Holy of Holies.) Finally, the third family, the family of Merari, pitched "on the side of the tabernacle northward" (Num. 3:35). They dealt with the hardware of the tabernacle—the wooden frames, the bars, the sockets of metal and so forth (Num. 3:36-37). Moses and the priests, incidentally, pitched on the east side of the tabernacle (the side to which the opening of the tabernacle faced), thus completing the square.

We should not be at all surprised, therefore, that the Levites' cities were allotted on the basis of these three family units. The Kohathites got the first lot. The priests themselves (the children of Aaron who belonged to this family) received thirteen cities (Josh. 21:19). The rest of this family received ten cities (Josh. 21:26). Gershon then received thirteen cities (Josh. 21:33) and Merari twelve (Josh. 21:40). All in all, forty-eight cities out of the land were given to the tribe of Levi (Josh. 21:41). God had commanded through Moses, "So all the cities which ye shall give to the Levites shall be forty and eight cities: them shall ye give with their suburbs" (Num. 35:7). Joshua's generation carried this out perfectly in the flow of continuity. To tamper with the unity of the Old Testament is to deal with it unfairly, not according to its own claims. The result is to make it intellectually meaningless.

The Cities of Refuge

The Levites' cities were divided into two parts: Six of the forty-eight cities were *cities of refuge*. God had commanded in the Pentateuch, "Among the cities which ye shall give unto the Levites there shall be six cities for refuge, which ye shall appoint for the manslayer, that he may flee thither: and to them ye shall add forty and two cities" (Num. 35:6). "The LORD also spake unto Joshua, saying, Speak to the children of Israel, saying, Appoint out for you cities of refuge, whereof I spake unto you by the hand of Moses" (Josh. 20:1-2). So Joshua set up the cities of refuge when he divided the land.

On Mount Sinai God gave the moral law. "God spake all these words . . ." and then came the Ten Commandments (Ex. 20:1-17). Immediately after this the civil law was given. As the race became a nation they needed a civil law, so God gave them one. The civil law for the Jews was based as much on the command of God as was the moral law.

One of the civil laws God gave was this: "He that smiteth a man, so that he die, shall be surely put to death. And if a man lie not in wait, but God deliver him into his hand; then I will appoint thee a place whither he shall flee" (Ex. 21: 12-13). If a man was a real murderer, he was to die; but a system was to be set up whereby a man who had slain somebody by mistake would not be put to death but would have a place of escape.

These cities of refuge are next mentioned in Numbers 35, to which I will return in a moment, and then in Deuteronomy 4:41-43, which names the three cities of refuge Moses established on the east side of Jordan. The next mention is in Deuteronomy 19. Since there is an interplay between Deuteronomy 19 and Joshua 20, I want to cite first some verses from that chapter of Joshua:

> The LORD also spake unto Joshua, saying, Speak to
> the children of Israel, saying, Appoint out for you
> cities of refuge, whereof I spake unto you by the hand
> of Moses: that the slayer that killeth any person una-
> wares and unwittingly may flee thither: and they shall
> be your refuge from the avenger of blood. And when
> he that doth flee unto one of those cities shall stand at
> the entering of the gate of the city, and shall declare
> his cause in the ears of the elders of that city, they shall
> take him into the city unto them, and give him a place,
> that he may dwell among them. And if the avenger of
> blood pursue after him, then they shall not deliver the
> slayer up into his hand; because he smote his neigh-
> bour unwittingly, and hated him not beforetime. And
> he shall dwell in that city, until he stand before the con-
> gregation for judgment, and until the death of the
> high priest that shall be in those days: then shall the
> slayer return, and come unto his own city, and unto his
> own house, unto the city from whence he fled....
> These were the cities appointed for all the children of
> Israel, and for the stranger that sojourneth among
> them, that whosoever killeth any person at unawares
> might flee thither, and not die by the hand of the
> avenger of blood, until he stood before the congrega-
> tion. (Josh. 20:1-6, 9)

This section obviously takes a lot for granted. If we only had
Joshua 20, we would wonder about much of the detail. Why
didn't God tell Joshua to give the people more information?
He did not have to because the people knew Deuteronomy
19, and there the details are enumerated with great clarity
and care:

> When the LORD thy God hath cut off the nations,
> whose land the LORD thy God giveth thee, and thou
> succeedest them, and dwellest in their cities, and in
> their houses; thou shalt separate three cities for thee in

the midst of thy land, which the LORD thy God giveth thee to possess it. Thou shalt prepare thee a way [that is, you shall build a road], and divide the coasts of thy land, which the LORD thy God giveth thee to inherit, into three parts, that every slayer may flee thither.

And this is the case of the slayer, which shall flee thither, that he may live: Whoso killeth his neighbour ignorantly, whom he hated not in time past; as when a man goeth into the wood with his neighbour to hew wood, and his hand fetcheth a stroke with the ax to cut down the tree, and the head slippeth from the helve, and lighteth upon his neighbour, that he die; he shall flee unto one of those cities, and live: lest the avenger of the blood pursue the slayer, while his heart is hot, and overtake him, because the way is long, and slay him; whereas he was not worthy of death, inasmuch as he hated him not in time past. Wherefore I command thee, saying, Thou shalt separate three cities for thee. And if the LORD thy God enlarge thy coast, as he hath sworn unto thy fathers, and give thee all the land which he promised to give unto thy fathers; if thou shalt keep all these commandments to do them, which I command thee this day, to love the LORD thy God, and to walk ever in his ways; then shalt thou add three cities more for thee, beside these three: that innocent blood be not shed in thy land, which the LORD thy God giveth thee for an inheritance, and so blood be upon thee.

But if any man hate his neighbour, and lie in wait for him, and rise up against him, and smite him mortally that he die, and fleeth into one of these cities: then the elders of his city shall send and fetch him thence, and deliver him into the hand of the avenger of blood, that he may die. Thine eye shall not pity him, but thou shalt put away the guilt of innocent blood from Israel, that it may go well with thee. (Deut. 19:1-13)

The cities of refuge did not help a real murderer. They pertained only to the man who had, unhappily, killed someone unintentionally. They were to aid the one who had committed an accidental homicide—and no one else. The text tells us why such a man had to flee. The state did not kill in the case of a homicide; it was the dead man's family who killed. The Bedouins follow the same practice to this day. If somebody kills a member of a family, someone is appointed by the family to be the *avenger of blood.* It is his right to go out and take the other man's life. But when a man has killed someone accidentally, and another man is coming to take his life, what shall he do? He shall run to a city of refuge. The city of refuge was for the accidental homicide fleeing from the avenger of blood.

Now we turn back to Numbers 35:

And the suburbs of the cities, which ye shall give unto the Levites, shall reach from the wall of the city and outward a thousand cubits round about. And ye shall measure from without the city on the east side two thousand cubits, and on the south side two thousand cubits, and on the west side two thousand cubits, and on the north side two thousand cubits; and the city shall be in the midst: this shall be to them the suburbs of the cities. . . .

These six cities shall be a refuge, both for the children of Israel, and for the stranger, and for the sojourner among them: that every one that killeth any person unawares may flee thither. And if he smite him with an instrument of iron, so that he die, he is a murderer: the murderer shall surely be put to death. And if he smite him with throwing a stone, wherewith he may die, and he die, he is a murderer: the murderer shall surely be put to death. Or if he smite him with an hand weapon of wood, werewith he may die, and he die, he is a murderer: the murderer shall surely be put to death. The revenger of blood himself shall slay the murderer: when he meeteth him, he shall slay him.

But if he thrust him of hatred, or hurl at him by laying of wait, that he die; or in enmity smite him with his hand, that he die: he that smote him shall surely be put to death; for he is a murderer: the revenger of blood shall slay the murderer, when he meeteth him. But if he thrust him suddenly without enmity, or have cast upon him any thing without laying of wait, or with any stone, wherewith a man may die, seeing him not, and cast it upon him, that he die, and was not his enemy, neither sought his harm: then the congregation shall judge between the slayer and the revenger of blood according to these judgments: and the congregation shall deliver the slayer out of the hand of the revenger of blood, and the congregation shall restore him to the city of his refuge, whither he was fled: and he shall abide in it unto the death of the high priest, which was anointed with the holy oil. But if the slayer shall at any time come without the border of the city of his refuge, whither he was fled; and the revenger of blood find him without the borders of the city of his refuge, and the revenger of blood kill the slayer; he shall not be guilty of blood: because he should have remained in the city of his refuge until after the death of the high priest: but after the death of the high priest the slayer shall return into the land of his possession.

So these things shall be for a statute of judgment unto you throughout your generations in all your dwellings. Whoso killeth any person, the murderer shall be put to death by the mouth of witnesses: but one witness shall not testify against any person to cause him to die. (Num. 35:4-5, 15-30)

It is really beautiful that the cities were available not only for the children of Israel but also for both the non-Israelites who were living permanently in the land and those who were merely passing through. This was entirely new to the heathen world. Here was real justice—a universal and civil code that pertained equally to the citizen and the stranger. This justice was not rooted in the notion of a superior people but in the character of God; therefore, it pertained to all men.

Moses told how to distinguish between an intentional murderer and an unwitting killer. A deliberate homicide involved a prepared instrument, a clear intent and a clear motive. Such a murderer had no place of refuge. But if a man thrust a victim "suddenly without enmity" or "cast any thing upon him without lying in wait" he had a place. For example, if a man was prying out a big rock and it accidentally fell on somebody coming along the path, this was not murder. It was without preparation and without motive.

In our jurisprudence, we follow in general the same procedure. In considering whether a man is guilty, our trials take into account the same questions. Moses clearly outlined the procedure. If a man killed somebody without premeditation, he was to run to a city of refuge! He was kept there until the facts were gathered (more than one witness was needed) and then he was tried, as in our jury system, by his peers. Not some great person but the assembled congregation decided whether he had committed murder or not. If he had, he was pushed outside the city where the avenger of blood could take his life. If he had not, he was returned to the city of refuge. He then had to remain in the city until the death of the current high priest or the protection was gone.

Law in a Post-Christian Culture

We can now begin to understand why it may be emphasized that in Reformation countries the Old Testament civil law has been the basis of our civil law. We are not a theocracy, it is true; nevertheless, when Reformation Christianity provided the consensus, men naturally looked back to the civil law that God gave Israel, not to carry it out in every detail but to see it as a pattern and a base.

But we have changed, of course. We are no longer a Christian culture. And because of that we are seeing a change in our concept of law. The differences between past and present fall into two areas.

The first difference involves the foundation of law. The cities of refuge were levitical cities, that is, they had something to do with God. The person taking refuge had to stay in the city until the death of the high priest so he would be reminded that the civil laws were related to God. They did not just exist in a sociological vacuum. Unlike modern man, the people of the Old Testament and of Christian communities after the Reformation did not view civil law as basically sociological. To them it was not founded primarily on a social contract. Civil law was related to society, but not only to society. It was ultimately related to the existence and character of God. This is important. Law which comes from God can provide something fixed. Today's sociological law is relativistic.

The *moral* law is rooted in the fact of the existence and character of God. It has validity because God is there. "And God spake all these words, saying, I am the LORD thy God, which have brought thee out of the land of Egypt, out of the house of bondage. Thou shalt have no other gods before me" (Ex. 20:1-3). The *civil* law is also based upon the reality of God's existence, so it, too, has an absolute base. Reformation law was like this—one can think of Samuel Rutherford's *Lex Rex*—in total contrast to the post-Christian, sociological law which is developing in the Western world.

Paul Robert, who lived at the end of the last century, was a wonderful Christian and a great Swiss painter of his era. He painted huge murals, one of which is on the stairwell of the old supreme court building in Lausanne, Switzerland. Paul Robert placed it there so the justices would never forget the basis of law. He knew what he was doing in every de-

193

tail, including the title, "Justice Instructing the Judges." We may not completely like his technique, because it is marked by the conventions of the period, but the mural has a strong thrust. Several litigants stand in the foreground of the painting: wife against husband, builder against architect. The question is, On what basis are the judges able to judge? Justice points with her sword so that the judges can follow it and see what should be the basis. Justice points to a book on which Robert has carefully lettered the phrase, *The Law of God.* That is tremendous! There was a foundation for civil law, fixed in the existence and character of God and his revelation of that character to men.

The second difference between the civil law of the theocracy and the law of the post-Christian world is the former's emphasis on the seriousness of murder. God commanded, "He that smiteth a man, so that he die, shall be surely put to death" (Ex. 21:12). Nothing could change this. No bribe or satisfaction—common practices in those days— could be taken for the murderer (Num. 35:31-32). As far back as the covenant with Noah, God said, "Whoso sheddeth man's blood, by man shall his blood be shed: for in the image of God made he man" (Gen. 9:6). The Bible says that though man is fallen he is still the image-bearer of God. Human worth does not rest on the fact that man can breed with others of the same biological species. Rather, it rests on the fact that man is unique; he is made in the image of God.

Man is a significant creature. He is not part of the machinery. And this has many implications. One which society must understand is that murder is not trivial but extremely serious. It is not merely a breach of social custom or mores, or even that which upsets society. The Bible's great outcry against the murderer is, "You have slain an image-bearer of God." When a person deliberately murders an image-bearer of God, he has done a serious thing indeed.

Because God exists and because he has a character, we live in a true moral universe. Murder breaks the law of the universe. This means that the murderer has true moral guilt before God—something our modern generation knows nothing or little about—and this guilt must be taken seriously.

We must keep saying to our generation that men are guilty with true moral guilt before a holy God, for the existential theologians who now control the theological thinking among both progressive Roman Catholics and liberal Protestants have no real sense of the importance of God's being there and his giving propositional truth in the Bible.

We must, therefore, respond forcefully that everything hangs not upon "God words" but upon the fact that God is really there and really has a character. He is really a holy God. Therefore, when I sin, my guilt is real. And because God is infinite, and infinitely holy, my guilt when I sin is total. The value of the guilt does not rest upon my value but upon the value of the one against whom I have sinned. Therefore, because I have sinned against the one who is infinitely holy, my guilt comes up to this level. True moral guilt has nothing to do with our finitude. If we see the tension as modern theologians and philosophers do between man (finite) and God (infinite), we can never derive true moral guilt. The law does not stand behind God, because the final thing is God. And it is God's character which *is* the law of the universe.

Christ and the Cities of Refuge

If we begin to tamper with the truth about true moral guilt, we will not be able to understand the death of Christ any more than we can understand the cities of refuge. In fact, we will understand it less. We would not want to take the cities of refuge as a type, but they certainly are a strong illustration of the work of Christ. It seems to me that the New Testament itself relates the work of Christ to these cities. Hebrews says,

For men verily swear by the greater: and an oath for

confirmation is to them an end of all strife. Wherein God, willing more abundantly to shew unto the heirs of promise the immutability of his counsel, confirmed it by an oath: that by two immutable things, in which it was impossible for God to lie, we might have a strong consolation, *who have fled for refuge to lay hold upon the hope set before us:* which hope we have as an anchor of the soul, both sure and stedfast, and which entereth into that within the vail; whither the forerunner is for us entered, even Jesus, made an high priest for ever after the order of Melchisedec. (Heb. 6:16-20)

In our study of the Gibeonites we discussed this passage's teaching about how seriously God takes an oath given in his name and about the surety of our safety in Christ. Now I would like us to consider the phrase *who have fled for refuge to lay hold upon the hope set before us.* In my opinion, although there is no way to be final about it, the writer of Hebrews, who is writing to Jews and is constantly referring to the Old Testament, is referring here to the cities of refuge and paralleling them to Christ's work.

Let us notice some facts about the cities of refuge. First, they were in central places on both sides of the Jordan, so they were easy to reach from any place in the country. God expressly commanded that roads were to be made to these cities (Deut. 19:3). From nonbiblical sources we can add some further detail about the highways. They were carefully repaired every spring, after the rains and bad weather of winter. Further, bridges were built where needed so that a man did not have to run down into a ravine but could go straight across, taking the shortest possible route to the city. At every crossroad were special signs which said, "Refuge! Refuge!" and pointed in the direction of the city. They had to be large enough so that a man running hard could easily read them.

We can picture a man coming up the road. Another man is pursuing him, sword out. The first man, having no time to use a magnifying glass, approaches the sign and sees the big words, "Refuge! Refuge!" He runs to the city and is safe.

Second, the cities of refuge were open to all—to the Israelite, the stranger and the sojourner.

Third, from nonbiblical sources we hear that the great doors of these cities were never locked. We can see why. Otherwise a man might die while beating on the door.

Fourth, these sources also tell us that each city of refuge was stocked with food. It was a sufficient refuge, then, not only providing legal protection but also meeting a man's needs once he was inside.

Fifth, we know from the Bible itself, of course, that if a killer did not flee to a city of refuge there was no help for him.

The similarities between the cities of refuge and Christ our refuge are striking. We can compare them point for point. First, Christ is easy to reach. We may cast ourselves upon Christ at any time, in any place. The church is to be the teller of this good news. The church is to cry, "Refuge! Refuge!" to the lost world. This emphasis is made at the very end of the Bible in the book of Revelation: "And the Spirit and the bride say, Come. And let him that heareth say, Come. And let him that is athirst come. And whosoever will, let him take the water of life freely" (Rev. 22:17).

Second, Christ is open to all—the Jew and the Gentile, the Greek and the barbarian, to all people.

Third, Christ never locks his gates. There is no need to wake him. He is infinite; he is God; he is never asleep. We do not have to beat upon the door and die because he does not open it. Many times I have stood by a deathbed and seen men believe in the last moments of life. It is good that there is no gate to unlock and that men can enter quickly.

Fourth, Christ is a totally sufficient refuge. Christ's death in space-time history is completely adequate to meet our need for refuge from the true moral guilt which we have. It is final because of who he is. He is the infinite second Person of the Trinity; therefore, his death has infinite value. Furthermore, the cities of refuge were not only a legal protection but also had a supply of food. So Christ not only makes a Christian legally safe through his propitiatory death, but he supplies the believer with great riches. God the Father is his father and the Holy Spirit indwells him and is the agent by which the whole Trinity produces Christ's fruit through him.

Fifth, if we do not flee to the refuge which God has given to us at such a great price, there is no help for us. Hebrews relates this negative emphasis to the Old Testament: "He that despised Moses' law died without mercy under two or three witnesses: of how much sorer punishment, suppose ye, shall he be thought worthy, who hath trodden under foot the Son of God, and hath counted the blood of the covenant, wherewith he was sanctified, an unholy thing, and hath done despite unto the Spirit of grace?" (Heb. 10: 28-29). There is not one of us who does not stand in that situation. We have heard the gospel, and, if in the Old Testament ignoring God's law brought death, what about us if we despise the work of Christ and the grace which he showers upon us?

But there are differences between the cities of refuge and Christ our refuge. The biggest difference is that the cities protected only the innocent. They were only for the man who killed by mistake. Christ died for the guilty, for the deliberate sinner. Who is that deliberate sinner? Every one of us can say, "It is I!"

How is it possible that the holy God would accept those that are guilty? It is not by giving up his holiness. He does not devalue that, or we would have no moral absolute in the universe. Rather, the reason Christ is able to be our redeemer is that he is a high priest and the sacrifice he gave was his own death. A man stayed in a city of refuge until the death of the high priest. Christ is our high priest. He has died once for all, and he lives forever. So, though we are legally guilty before the God who is there, when we cast ourselves upon him we are free forever. Hebrews says this strongly:

And they truly were many priests, because they were not suffered to continue by reason of death: but this man, because he continueth ever, hath an unchangeable priesthood. Wherefore he is able also to save them to the uttermost that come unto God by him, seeing he ever liveth to make intercession for them. For such an high priest became us, who is holy, harmless, undefiled, separate from sinners, and made higher than the heavens; who needeth not daily, as those high priests, to offer up sacrifice, first for his own sins, and then for the people's: for this he did once, when he offered up himself. (Heb. 7:23-27)

Hebrews also speaks of Christ as "the forerunner [who] is for us entered" (Heb. 6:20). That means that he has entered into God's presence and that we can enter, too. When do we enter this refuge? I would suggest we enter at three different times. First, we enter in once for all at the moment we cast ourselves upon Christ and accept him as our Savior. We are declared justified by God the Judge on the basis of Christ's finished work. In Romans 5:11 Paul uses the aorist tense, indicating our justification is a past thing, completed forever. If we are saved, we are saved. Second, we enter into this refuge as Christians in every existential moment when we claim the blood of Christ to cover a specific sin. Third, at that great moment when we die or when the Lord returns we will enter in perfectly and completely.

The second difference between Christ and a city of refuge is that, happily, Christ is nearer than any city of refuge. A runner could fail, but a man who looks to Christ can never fail. The Bible makes a specific promise, "Him that cometh to me I will in no wise cast out" (John 6:37). In fact, Jesus says, "I stand at the door and knock" (Rev. 3:20). He himself seeks us.

We are not like a man who runs to a city of refuge and is acquitted after a trial because he is innocent. We are guilty. If you are still a non-Christian, run to Christ, for God's own promises say, "Refuge! Refuge!" If we are Christians, we should take Christ as our sufficient refuge in bringing specific sins under the work of Christ and in all the vicissitudes of life, this moment and moment by moment through the whole of our lives.

twelve
Joshua's Farewell: Choose!

The major campaigns of conquest were over. The land had been divided and the cities of refuge established. "And it came to pass a long time after that the LORD had given rest unto Israel from all their enemies round about, that Joshua waxed old and stricken in age. And Joshua called for all Israel, and for their elders, and for their heads, and for their judges, and for their officers" (Josh. 23:1-2).

What would Joshua say to the people at such a time? What was his word to them as they were about to continue without his leadership? He began like this:

I am old and stricken in age: and ye have seen all that the LORD your God hath done unto all these nations because of you; for the LORD your God is he that hath fought for you. Behold, I have divided unto you by lot these nations that remain, to be an inheritance for your tribes, from Jordan, with all the nations that I have cut off, even unto the great sea westward. And the LORD your God, he shall expel them from before you, and drive them from out of your sight; and ye

> shall possess their land, as the LORD your God hath
> promised unto you. (Josh. 23:2-5)

Joshua gave a promise for the future which was rooted in a
space-time past. He did not ask the people to make a Kier-
kegaardian leap of faith. This stress on God's action in history recurs throughout his farewell:

> And, behold, this day I am going the way of all the
> earth: and ye know in all your hearts and in all your
> souls, that not one thing hath failed of all the good
> things which the LORD your God spake concerning
> you; all are come to pass unto you, and not one thing
> hath failed thereof. . . . And when they cried unto the
> LORD, he put darkness between you and the Egyp-
> tians, and brought the sea upon them, and covered
> them; and your eyes have seen what I have done in
> Egypt: and ye dwelt in the wilderness a long season. . . .
> For the LORD our God, he it is that brought us up and
> our fathers out of the land of Egypt, from the house of
> bondage, and which did those great signs in our sight,
> and preserved us in all the way wherein we went, and
> among all the people through whom we passed. (Josh.
> 23:14; 24:7, 17)

Joshua appealed to what some of the people had seen themselves. The former generation had died, but some who
heard Joshua's farewell had been children when the Israelites crossed the Red Sea. He reminded them of the historical realities on which their faith rested. Biblical faith is rooted in what may be seen by the eye and heard by the ear. The
difference between Greek and Hebrew thinking is not that
the Greeks were rationalists while the Hebrews were exis-
tentialists. Quite the contrary. The Jews insisted on a
tougher reality than the Greeks: They demanded not only
that which was reasonable but also that which was rooted in
space and time.

This emphasis continues in the New Testament, which
insists, for instance, that the first eleven chapters of Genesis

describe actual history. Every New Testament reference to these chapters in Genesis indicates that the event mentioned was space-time history. The New Testament also assumes that that history is stated in ordinary literary forms. Scripture never suddenly confronts us with a heavenly language which carries us into a contentless religious experience.

Believers have been given good and sufficient reasons for believing. This was not only true in Joshua's day; it has been true throughout God's redemptive program. When John explains why he wrote his gospel he says that "many other space-time proofs did Jesus in the presence of his disciples which are not written in this book" (John 20:30). "Space-time proofs" is exactly what the Greek word means in the terminology of our own day. John's statement parallels what Joshua said. What happened at the Red Sea was done in the Israelites' presence. Jesus' actions, recorded in John's Gospel, were done in the presence of the disciples. These space-time proofs were written, John continues, "that ye might believe that Jesus is the Christ, the Son of God: and that believing ye might have life through his name" (John 20:31). So whether it is in Joshua's exhortation or through the cry of John's Gospel, the Bible claims that there are good and sufficient reasons for faith that may be considered and acted upon.

Joshua was saying to the people as he was about to leave them, "Remember the past! Remember these things that are rooted in history and open to reason!"

Remember the Standard

The promises for the future were not, however, unconditional. Joshua confronted the people with a set of categories within which they had to live if the promises were to come to pass: "Be ye therefore very courageous to keep and to do all that is written in the book of the law of Moses, that ye turn not aside therefrom to the right hand or to the left"

(Josh. 23:6). This hearkens back to Joshua 1 and its emphasis upon the book: "This book of the law shall not depart out
of thy mouth; but thou shalt meditate therein day and
night, that thou mayest observe to do according to all that is
written therein: for then thou shalt make thy way prosperous, and then thou shalt have good success" (Josh. 1:8). The
statement God made to Joshua at the beginning of his leadership, Joshua passed on to the people at the end of his life,
namely, "live within the categories of the book and you will
be blessed."

At the end of Joshua's life we see once more the growth of
the canon: "And Joshua wrote these words in the book of
the law of God" (Josh. 24:26). Moses' books were accepted
as normative at the time of his death, and by the time Joshua
died he had written another book and added it to the canon
which was the authority for God's people. This is in complete contrast to the new theology with its focus in contentless existential experience. God gave the people a set of
moral categories in verbalized form, categories that God
himself declared to be absolute. Joshua said, "This is the
standard! If you depart from it, the conditional portions
of the promise will come to an end." God himself gave a
written objective propositional authority by which to judge
in moral matters.

Joshua contrasted what would happen if the people lived
within these categories with what would happen if they did
not:

> One man of you shall chase a thousand: for the LORD
> your God, he it is that fighteth for you, as he hath
> promised you. Take good heed therefore unto your-
> selves, that ye love the LORD your God. Else if ye do in
> any wise go back, and cleave unto the remnant of these
> nations, even these that remain among you, and shall
> make marriages with them, and go in unto them, and
> they to you: know for a certainty that the LORD your
> God will no more drive out any of these nations from

before you; but they shall be snares and traps unto you, and scourges in your sides, and thorns in your eyes, until ye perish from off this good land which the LORD your God hath given you. (Josh. 23:10-13)
This carries us back to Ebal and Gerizim, where Joshua "read all the words of the law, the blessings and cursings, according to all that is written in the book of the law. There was not a word of all that Moses commanded, which Joshua read not before all the congregation of Israel, with the women, and the little ones, and the strangers that were conversant among them" (Josh. 8:34-35). These commands, considered simple and straightforward enough for everyone, young or old, Israelite or non-Israelite, to understand, highlighted the conditional aspects of the Abrahamic covenant. So at the end of his life Joshua was insisting, as he had practiced, that the blessings depended upon whether or not the people kept God's commands. Once we depart from this mentality, we are on totally shifting sand. God's Word, the Bible, is a rock, something solid and immovable. It gives us moral absolutes rather than situation, relativistic ethics.

An Ungodly Heritage

Joshua gathered all the tribes at Shechem, one of the cities of refuge. He began by reminding them, "Thus sayeth the LORD God of Israel, Your fathers dwelt on the other side of the flood [that is, the Euphrates River] in old time, even Terah, the father of Abraham, and the father of Nachor: and they served other gods" (Josh. 24:2). We know that Ur and Haran were centers of moon worship. Joshua was telling the people, "Your past heritage is a people that were not God's people."

Ezekiel likewise points this out: "Thus saith the Lord GOD unto Jerusalem; thy birth and thy nativity is of the land of Canaan; thy father was an Amorite, and thy mother an Hittite" (Ezek. 16:3). No compliment to a Jew, certainly! Nevertheless, Ezekiel told the people, "That's what you were. The only reason you are something else is that God in his grace reached down and did something with you."

God does not allow Christians, either, to go on in pride. He constantly reminds us of our heritage—a heritage of those who have turned aside from him. In Ephesians Paul says to believers, "Wherein in time past ye walked according to the course of this world, according to the prince of the power of the air, the spirit that now worketh in the children of disobedience: among whom also we all had our conversation in times past in the lusts of our flesh, fulfilling the desires of the flesh and of the mind; and were by nature the children of wrath, even as others" (Eph. 2:2-3). Who does he say we were? He says to us, "Remember, at one time Satan was your god and your father. This is who you were."

Whether studying the Old Testament or the New, we are reminded that we are not where we are because of a long, wise and godly heritage. We come from rebellion. Individually, we are children of wrath. After we are Christians, we must look at others who are still under God's wrath and always say, "I am essentially what you are. If I am in a different place, it is not because I am intrinsically better than you, but simply because God has done something in my life." There is no place for pride.

Three Sets of Gods

In reminding the Israelites of their ungodly heritage, Joshua spoke of three sets of false gods and called upon the people to choose against them:

And Joshua said unto all the people, Thus saith the LORD God of Israel, Your fathers dwelt on the other side of the flood in old time, even Terah, the father of Abraham, and the father of Nachor: and they served other gods. And I took your father Abraham from the other side of the flood, and led him throughout all the land of Canaan, and multiplied his seed, and gave him Isaac. And I gave unto Isaac Jacob and Esau:

and I gave unto Esau mount Seir, to possess it; but Jacob and his children went down into Egypt. I sent Moses also and Aaron, and I plagued Egypt, according to that which I did among them: and afterward I brought you out. And I brought your fathers out of Egypt: and ye came unto the sea; and the Egyptians pursued after your fathers with chariots and horsemen unto the Red sea. And when they cried unto the LORD, he put darkness between you and the Egyptians; and brought the sea upon them, and covered them; and your eyes have seen what I have done in Egypt: and ye dwelt in the wilderness a long season. And I brought you into the land of the Amorites, which dwelt on the other side Jordan; and they fought with you: and I gave them into your hand, that ye might possess their land; and I destroyed them from before you. (Josh. 24:2-8)

Interestingly, the three sets of gods were related to three different waters. On the other side of the Euphrates were the gods of the Sumerian and Babylonian culture. On the other side of the Red Sea were the gods of ancient Egypt. Across the river Jordan were the gods of the Amorites.

Now therefore [Joshua challenged] fear the LORD and serve him in sincerity and in truth: and put away the gods which your fathers served on the other side of the flood, and in Egypt; and serve ye the LORD. And if it seem evil unto you to serve the LORD, choose you this day whom ye will serve; whether the gods which your fathers served that were on the other side of the flood, or the gods of the Amorites, in whose land ye dwell: but as for me and my house, we will serve the LORD. (Josh. 24:14-15)

"Choose," he said, "between the Sumerian gods, the Egyptian gods, the Amorite gods—and the Lord Choose!"

Joshua's own choice was emphatic· "But as for me and my house, we will serve the Lord." The English uses a future tense here, but the Hebrew tense has a fuller meaning. It expresses continuous action. It involves the future, but it also can point to the past. Joshua was undoubtedly affirming, "I have chosen, and I will choose."

His words were not just an empty boast because the people standing in front of him knew his past choices. Not long after the crossing of the Red Sea, Joshua had stood as the general against the Amalekites. When the people worshiped the golden calf, Joshua, by choice, did not identify with them. He stood with Caleb against his own people when they were wrong. He chose to affirm that God's word was valid and that they could conquer the land. When God's leader, Moses, died outside the promised land, Joshua knew it was because God had clearly told Moses to do one thing and Moses had done another. He saw the result of Moses' bad choice.

This was the character of Joshua. He chose, and he chose, and he chose, and he kept right on choosing. He understood the dynamics of choice—once-for-all choice and existential choice as well. Thus his word to the people was not an affirmation puffed up on the spur of the moment. It was deeply imbedded in Joshua's comprehension of what is required of a person made in the image of God, one called upon not to obey God like a machine or an animal, but to obey God by choice.

The people responded positively to Joshua's challenge:
God forbid that we should forsake the LORD, to serve other gods; for the LORD our God, he it is that brought us up and our fathers out of the land of Egypt, from the house of bondage, and which did those great signs in our sight, and preserved us in all the way wherein we went, and among all the people through whom we passed: and the LORD drave out from before us all the people, even the Amorites which dwelt in the land: therefore will we also serve the LORD; for he is our God. (Josh. 24:16-18)

Because of what the people had seen in the past, they made the same choice as Joshua. Yet theirs was in one respect different. Joshua's choice was rooted in a series of continuous choices. These people had been like a weathervane. Consequently, Joshua warned them not to choose lightly:

And Joshua said unto the people, Ye cannot serve the LORD: for he is an holy God; he is a jealous God; he will not forgive your transgressions nor your sins. If ye forsake the LORD, and serve strange gods, then he will turn and do you hurt, and consume you, after that he hath done you good. And the people said unto Joshua, Nay; but we will serve the LORD. And Joshua said unto the people, Ye are my witnesses against yourselves that ye have chosen you the LORD, to serve him. And they said, We are witnesses. Now therefore put away, said he, the strange gods which are among you, and incline your heart unto the LORD God of Israel. And the people said unto Joshua, The LORD our God will we serve, and his voice will we obey. (Josh. 24: 19-24)

Despite Joshua's warning, the people continued to insist. So Joshua stressed that their choice (which was, of course, the right choice) had to be total and have practical repercussions in their lives.

The Extension of the Covenant

In response to the people's affirmation, the covenant was extended another step: "So Joshua made a covenant with the people that day, and set them a statute and an ordinance in Shechem" (Josh. 24:25). This covenant was a part of the ongoing covenant. You will remember, it had been established immediately after the Fall and was continued in the times of Noah, Abraham and Moses. At the end of Joshua's life, it was again extended. This extension of the covenant was related to the book: "And Joshua wrote these words in the book of the law of God, and took a great stone, and set it up there under an oak, that was by the sanctuary of the LORD. And Joshua said unto all the people, Behold, this stone shall be a witness unto us; for it hath heard all the words of the LORD which he spake unto us: it shall be therefore a witness unto you, lest ye deny your God" (Josh. 24:26-27).

Notice Joshua put up a stone as a testimony. Now, in addition to the stones at Gilgal and the altar on Ebal, another memorial in stone was established so that in years to come the children of this generation would be able to walk through the land and be reminded of what occurred in that place and of the promises their fathers had made to God.

Sometime after the covenant was extended, Joshua died:

And it came to pass after these things, that Joshua the son of Nun, the servant of the LORD, died, being an hundred and ten years old. And they buried him in the border of his inheritance in Timnath-serah, which is in mount Ephraim, on the north side of the hill of Gaash. And Israel served the LORD all the days of Joshua, and all the days of the elders that overlived Joshua, and which had known all the works of the LORD that he had done for Israel. (Josh. 24:29-31)

The faithfulness of Joshua's generation is also extolled in the book of Judges, but it is followed by a shift:

And the people served the LORD all the days of Joshua, and all the days of the elders that outlived Joshua, who had seen all the great works of the LORD, that he did for Israel.... And also all that generation were gathered unto their fathers: and there arose another generation after them, which knew not the LORD, nor yet the works which he had done for Israel. (Judg. 2:7, 10)

We come to a group of people who did not imitate Joshua's continual choice. The children of Israel remembered for a time the choice they had made at Joshua's farewell, but they then forgot it. And thus came the confusion, the sorrow and the total lawlessness of the period of the judges.

We are seeing exactly the same shift in our own generation. Those of us from the Reformation countries have experienced a Christian consensus. (This does not mean that every individual was a Christian but that society was strongly influenced by Christian values.) But my generation and the generations immediately preceding me made a bad choice, and so we now live in a post-Christian world. The choices of faith have been set aside and forgotten, and, accordingly, the confusion, sorrow and lawlessness of the time of the judges is occurring in our generation. If you are a member of the younger generation, you are a recipient of the consequences of this bad choice. This is who you are. To understand yourself, you must understand that you have grown up in a post-Christian world.

Choices

The element of personal choice stands out as a key theme in the book of Joshua.

In chapter 2 of this study we saw that the captain of the host of the Lord stood before Joshua, and Joshua had to choose. The people of God had the opportunity to follow their own activisms and wisdom, but Joshua made a different decision for them. He fell down and said, "It's your leadership." And he removed his shoes in the presence of the One who had now come as the captain of the host of the LORD.

In chapter 3 we considered the blessings to the Jews under the national portion of the Abrahamic covenant. Under Joshua the people chose to enter the land (a complete contrast to the choice they made thirty-eight years before) and suddenly, after all the decades of waiting, the complex of the Abrahamic covenant fell into place. We also saw that, as Romans 9—11 make clear, the Jews' whole history, from that time to this and into the future, rests on their choices. If they continued in disobedience and unbelief, they did not have God's blessing. If they obeyed, they came into the blessing of the people of God.

Rahab and the Gibeonites (chaps. 4 and 8) chose to step over among the people of God and entered into the spiritual portion of the Abrahamic covenant. Rahab the harlot became an ancestor of Jesus Christ. The Gibeonites, down to the time of David and beyond, worked close to the altar. All this because they had decided to step over from the kingdom of darkness to the kingdom of the living God!

Chapter 5 concerned two kinds of memorials, the stones and the sacraments. The Israelites chose to cross the river Jordan, enter the land and establish the stone memorials as God commanded. Joshua—foolishly from a human military point of view—observed the sacrament of circumcision. Then he observed the Passover. But we also saw that the external signs, like the sacraments of baptism and the Lord's Supper today, mean nothing unless there is a choice to be in a proper relationship with God. They are not mechanical.

In chapter 6 we saw Achan's titanic choice. This one man decided to take silver and gold and the mantle of Shinar. He coveted within; then he acted. Soon he saw the terrible results of his choice. He himself died, but others died, too. His choice led to a temporary defeat for the whole people of God.

On Mount Ebal and Mount Gerizim (chap. 7) a choice was set before the people: "Obey the propositional moral absolutes of God, and you'll receive blessing within the covenant. If you don't, the blessing will come to an end."

In chapter 9 we saw how Caleb chose to stand against the rest of the Israelites. We saw how the people failed to take the totality of the land because they lacked faith. But Caleb went in and took the territory he had been promised. The faith which he had exhibited through thirty-eight years of wandering plus seven years of conquest he continued to practice.

In chapter 10 we saw that the two and a half tribes that returned to the east side of Jordan chose to serve the true, living God. They even raised a great altar of testimony to show that they intended to continue to worship him proper-y even though they had left the west side of the river. The .emaining tribes chose to practice both truth and love as they dealt with what they feared was rebellion.

The cities of refuge involved two sorts of choices (chap. 11). The first sort of choice was made by the man who really chose to murder; the second was made by the innocent man who chose to flee to a city of refuge to escape the avenger of blood.

So we find throughout the entire book of Joshua an emphasis on choice—choice that makes a tremendous difference in history, for individuals, for groups, for future generations. The Bible insists, "Don't forget who you are. You are not a puppet or a machine. You do not obey a universal law of cause and effect in a closed system. Rather, you are made in the image of God, and, as such, you must choose, and choose rightly, at every point." Adam chose wrongly, and we all bear the marks of his error. Abraham believed God, and his choice was counted to him for righteousness. Joshua chose rightly, too. For those of us today, the situation is the same. Whether Christian or non-Christian, we are called upon to make choices which will have significant results.

If you are not a Christian, remember that you are faced with a choice which will make a total difference to you. God says to you concerning that choice,

And as Moses lifted up the serpent in the wilderness, even so must the Son of man be lifted up: that whosoever believeth in him should not perish, but have eternal life. For God so loved the world, that he gave his only begotten Son, that whosoever believeth in him should not perish, but have everlasting life. For God sent not his Son into the world to condemn the world; but that the world through him might be saved. He that believeth on him is not condemned: but he that believeth not is condemned already, because he hath not believed in the name of the only begotten Son of God.... He that believeth not the Son shall not see life; but the wrath of God abideth on him. (John 3: 14-18, 36)

Your choice is not a piece of theater. You are not thistle-down in the wind. There are good and sufficient reasons in history to know that this is the choice you should make, and you are called upon to make it. Choose once for all for justification.

If you are a Christian, having made the once-for-all choice that was involved in your justification, remember that your choices do not end. You do not enter a static situation. Paul gives this imperative, "If you live in the Spirit, walk in the Spirit" (Gal. 5:16). We must continually choose to live within the commands of God.

In Romans Paul describes himself as "a slave of Jesus Christ" (Rom. 1:1). In Philippians he pictures both Timothy and himself as "the slaves of Jesus Christ" (Phil. 1:1). Did Paul have to be a slave? No. A Roman slave could not escape, for he had a hard, heavy band of iron riveted around his neck. He could not remove it. Paul, by a continual act of choice, held the slave-band in place.

Joshua's great call "Choose! Choose!" is as meaningful to us today as to the people of God when Joshua was preparing to leave them. If you are a Christian, I urge you to continue to make this choice:

Now therefore fear the LORD, and serve him in sincerity and in truth: and put away the gods which your fathers served on the other side of the flood, and in Egypt; and serve ye the LORD. And if it seem evil unto you to serve the LORD, choose you this day whom ye will serve; whether the gods which your fathers served

that were on the other side of the flood, or the gods of
the Amorites, in whose land ye dwell: but as for me
and my house, we will serve the LORD. (Josh. 24:
14-15)

What are your gods of Ur? What are your gods of Egypt?
What are your gods of the Amorites? *What are your gods?*
What gods did you leave when you made the great first
choice to become a Christian? God says, "You chose once
for all to be a Christian. Fine. Continue to choose, continue
to choose, continue to choose—moment by moment, existentially. You must continue to choose between the old gods
and me, the living God." And, as Joshua said, you must not
choose lightly.

When the people affirmed their commitment to God,
Joshua insisted, "Remember how you have chosen" (Josh.
24:31). Joshua affirmed, "As for me and my house, we will
serve the Lord." Like Joshua, any Christian who wishes to
be of any help to this poor, sinful world, especially to a con-
fused generation like ours, must be one who continues to
choose to serve the Lord in the here and now. Let us say as
we face the choices of life: As for me and my house, by
God's grace, we will serve the Lord!